Acadian-Cajun
Genealogy
Step by Step

Acadian-Cajun Genealogy
Step by Step

by
Timothy Hebert

Published by The Center for Louisiana Studies
University of Southwestern Louisiana
Lafayette, Louisiana

Library of Congress Catalog Number: 93-74254
ISBN Number: 0-940984-87-3

Copyright 1993
University of Southwestern Louisiana

Published by The Center for Louisiana Studies
P.O. Box 40831
University of Southwestern Louisiana
Lafayette, LA   70504-0831

CONTENTS

PREFACE..*ix*

INTRODUCTION..1
    How to Use This Book 1

Chapter 1 — ACADIAN-CAJUN ANCESTRY....................................3
    Table I: Acadian-Cajun Surnames...6

Chapter 2 — GENEALOGICAL RESEARCH.....................................9
    Genealogy Basics...9
    Where to Go.. 12
    Table II: Acadiana Area Courthouses..................................... 18
    Table III: Diocese of Louisiana—Archives 20
    Materials and Equipment... 24
    Types of Information 29

Chapter 3 — RESEARCH: 1921 to Today 33

Chapter 4 — RESEARCH: 1810 to 1920.. 39

Chapter 5 — RESEARCH: 1786 to 1809.. 53

Chapter 6 — RESEARCH: 1755 to 1785.. 59

Chapter 7 — RESEARCH: 1636 to 1754.. 66

Chapter 8 — PUTTING IT ALL TOGETHER................................... 70

APPENDIXES 73
    A: Helpful Hints 74
    B: Genealogy Forms.. 76
    C: Maps 79
    D: Reference Sources.. 84
    E: The History of Acadians-Cajuns.....................................113
    F: Acadian-Cajun Timeline 120
    G: Canadian and Louisiana Genealogical Societies
         and Their Periodicals..123
    H: Libraries with Significant Acadian-Cajun Resources...............127
    I: Genealogical Supply Companies.....................................135
    J: Louisiana Genealogical Travel Guide..............................138
    K: Acadian Genealogical Travel Guide 142

DEDICATION

I would like to thank my wife, Martha,
for putting up with all of my time spent on genealogy;

and I would like to dedicate this book to my parents,
Norman and Shirley Hebert,
and to their parents, and to their parents,
and to their parents, . . .

PREFACE

Did you ever wonder where you came from? No, I'm not talking about where you were born; I mean, where in the WORLD your ancestors lived? Who were they? . . . what countries did they come from? . . . why did they come here? . . . when did they get here? Obtaining answers to these questions brings you into the field of genealogy—the study of your "roots."

Genealogy is the study of your family tree . . . your ancestors (and descendants). Genealogical research is the process of finding those long-lost relatives. You can spend hours on it and not even notice the time go by. You may as well know now, your spouse will probably get to hate it because it will take up so much of your time. Once caught up in it, it can be a most time-consuming hobby. Finding an ancestor's name after hours of research using genealogical skills and clues can be just as satisfying as solving a good mystery. And it will be more interesting, since the mysteries being solved will relate to you.

Some people may wonder why knowledge about their ancestors is of any relevance. Well, it gives you a comfortable feeling to know the past . . . where, when, and why everything came together to produce *you*. It allows you to better relate to past world events to know where your family fit into them. If you have any Acadian or Cajun blood in you, this book should help you to identify your ancestors.

This book was written to share information I acquired the hard way. I have traced about 95% of my ancestors back to the Old World. There are many tricks and tips you pick up while accumulating that many ancestors. By following the outline in this book and using its advice, you can avoid many of the pitfalls of the beginning genealogist.

This book was also written in hopes that it will advance interest in Acadian and Cajun genealogy. The history of these people is too important to be forgotten. Most descendants of the Acadians have no idea what their forefathers went through. I hope that interest in their genealogy will bring more of these people (of which I am one) to an understanding of their heritage.

Acadian-Cajun
Genealogy
Step by Step

INTRODUCTION

HOW TO USE THIS BOOK

This book is not a basic how-to book on genealogy; neither is it a treatise on the Acadian or Cajun people. It is a mixture of the two . . . put together in a unique fashion. Once you have read about determining the possibility of your Acadian-Cajun ancestry in the next chapter, we will move on to some genealogy basics. When you are familiar with the tools, techniques, and sources to use, we will start going back in time.

You should familiarize yourself with the history of the areas in which you will be working. This will often help you in finding information. For example, knowing what happened to the Acadians during the deportations of 1755-1763 will help tell you where to look for records. A brief history of Acadia and south Louisiana is in the Appendix; but there are several books that go into much more detail. To get the most from the least amount of material, you may want to read:

Acadia: The Geography of Early Nova Scotia (Andrew Hill Clark) [covers Acadia up to the late 1700's],

Scattered to the Wind": Dispersal and Wanderings of the Acadians, 1755-1809 (Carl A. Brasseaux) [identifies the movements of the exiled Acadians]

The Founding of New Acadia (Carl A. Brasseaux) [emphasizes the movement of the Acadians and their resettlement in Louisiana]

Acadian to Cajun: Transformation of a People, 1803-1877 (Carl A. Brasseaux) [traces the cultural metamorphosis of the Louisiana Acadians]

Cajun Country (Ancelet, Edwards, and Pitre) [from the resettlement to modern times].

The complete references and other books are found in the Appendix. If you understand the history behind the genealogy, things will be easier for you and will make much more sense as you go back in time.

Each successive chapter will cover a specifically chosen time period. You will be guided through each time period while being told where to look and what information to look for. The resources are listed where applicable, as well as in the Appendix. There are five chapters covering the five different time periods. As you move through the book, you will be going back in time . . . ultimately reaching your Louisiana and European ancestors that settled Acadia back in the early 1600s and Louisiana in the 1700's. The final chapter tells you how to handle all of the information that you have compiled if you decide to put your efforts into print.

This book will not cover every type of research in great detail. It will concentrate on the most helpful types and those most likely to be undertaken by a beginning to intermediate genealogist. Advanced genealogical materials/techniques may be mentioned, but not thoroughly covered. There are many other books (such as *The Source*) that cover genealogical techniques in detail. Chapter 2 of this book will be a crash course in genealogy, specifically pointing out techniques you will need for Acadian-Cajun research. This book should enable you to identify most of your ancestors. Of course, we all run into a few "brick wall" ancestors (whose line suddenly stops) that need more sophisticated genealogical research. For those difficult problems, you should seek out more information on those specific areas. By the time you get that far, you will have been exposed to enough material that you will know where to go for help.

Don't forget about the Appendix. It contains a great deal of useful information. Refer to it as the text makes reference to it. The travel guide should be of great use if you ever travel to Louisiana or Canada to do research. It not only tells you where to go for Acadian-Cajun genealogical information, but it gives you ideas on other things you can do while there.

I

ACADIAN-CAJUN ANCESTRY

Like any area of study, genealogy is composed of a multitude of different areas . . . French, German, colonial, slaves, and so on. Your genealogy will probably be in several areas; and these areas may well overlap. Your great-great-grandparents may have been colonial, their parents—French colonial, their grandparents—French, their great-grandparents—French and German, and so on. This book, although it contains information that can be used in many areas of genealogy, is concentrated on helping you find Acadian and Cajun ancestors.

What are Acadian and Cajun ancestors? They are different, and yet they are the same. The Acadians were the settlers (mostly French) who colonized the area of Canada now known as the Maritime Provinces (Nova Scotia, New Brunswick, Prince Edward Island) in the seventeenth century. Many of them left or were deported (exiled) in the mid-eighteenth century to Canada, England, France, British colonies, and French colonies. Some moved from place to place, searching for a new home. By the year 1800, they had settled into their new homes and integrated (to various degrees) into the native populations. So, they became Canadians, French, Cajuns, etc. with an Acadian heritage. The bulk of pure Acadian research covered by this book, therefore, will cover the Acadians prior to the mass deportations (which ended about 1763). For Acadian information after the deportations and resettling, you will need to consult a reference work specializing in the area in which they settled. For example, if your Acadian ancestors remained in Canada (or returned to Canada after the exiles), you may want to refer to Angus Baxter's *In Search of Your Canadian Roots* to help you get back to the Acadians. More specifically, if they remained in Nova Scotia you should consult Terrence Punch's *Genealogical Research in Nova Scotia.* Likewise, if they settled elsewhere you should consult reference material devoted to that area.

The largest portion of Acadians exiled from the Canadian area settled in south Louisiana in the latter part of the eighteenth century. This book *will* cover those Acadians and other nationalities that became known as Cajuns. The word Cajun comes from a mispronunciation of Acadian, just as Injun is a mispronunciation of Indian. For the purposes of this book, we will refer to Cajuns as the people based in south Louisiana back to the year 1800. Before that, the different nationalities were still somewhat separate. After

3

1800, the mixture of Acadian, French, Canadian, Spanish, German, and a few other nationalities formed the Cajun people. They collectively became known as Cajuns (a derivative of the word Acadian) because the Acadians were the dominant culture. After a few generations, there were descendants of German and Spanish settlers speaking fluent Cajun French. This book will also cover those Louisiana settlers of the eighteenth century who eventually merged with the Acadians. A more detailed history of the Acadian people can be found in the Appendix.

Today people of Acadian-Cajun descent are found throughout the world. The largest populations are found in Louisiana (almost 1,000,000), Canada, and France. Even though your name may be Smith, Acadians or Cajuns could easily pop up in your ancestry. But how do you know if your own ancestry includes Acadians or Cajuns?

The best indicators are locations and surnames. If you have relatives who come from south Louisiana or southeastern Canada, it is quite possible that you have some Acadian and/or Cajun ancestry. If you come upon a "French-sounding" name, it could well be Acadian. Table I lists the most common Acadian and Cajun surnames. Please note that some "Cajun" names are not Acadian, since other nationalities joined with the Acadians to form the Cajun people. These non-Acadian Cajuns include surnames such as Lirette, Authement, and Falgout. You may want to check the list at this time to see how many of your lines are on the list. You usually do not have just one Acadian-Cajun surname. The people usually married within their own culture, so, if a certain relative is Acadian-Cajun, there is a good chance that many of his/her ancestors were, too.

Okay . . . so you believe that there *is* some Acadian-Cajun ancestry in your family. Congratulations! I've got good news. There are a couple of characteristics of the Acadian-Cajun people that make your genealogical search much easier.

First, they had a habit of staying in the same place and marrying people of the same heritage. The usual genealogical search for ancestors involves searching in many areas, often scattered about the country. More often than not, this is not the case with Acadian-Cajun ancestors. This means, with the proper background material, one can go into a well-equipped Acadian-Cajun genealogical library and come out the same day with a couple of hundred years of ancestors! People of other heritages may easily find that ancestors come from several different states. If your ancestors are Acadian-Cajun, most of them may have lived less than 100 miles from each other!

Any genealogist who has chased all over the country for ancestors (and there are many of them) can appreciate how lucky a person is to have an Acadian-Cajun ancestry. The scope of the search is often quite small compared with other genealogical areas.

The second reason to be thankful for Acadian-Cajun ancestry is their religion. All Acadians (seventeenth/eighteenth century) were Roman Catholic. Most Cajuns were Roman Catholic. As a matter of fact, Louisiana Acadian-Cajuns *had* to be Catholic until the United States purchased the Louisiana Territory. Under France and Spain, they were required to be Catholics because that was the state religion. Most of them continued as Catholics after Louisiana joined the United States. Protestantism did not reach significant numbers until the twentieth century. Even today, Roman Catholics still outnumber Protestants in south Louisiana. So, why is being Catholic of importance in genealogical work? Catholics kept good records . . . outstanding records compared to the Protestant religions. Church records of births, marriages, and deaths/funerals can be found all the way back to the early 1700s. *And*, most of the pre-twentieth-century Catholic records have been published in book form. Instead of running all around south Louisiana in search of individual records, one can find a complete set of early church records in a good library. Of course, the church records are incomplete . . . with gaps and exclusions; but they still contain a vast amount of information that may be hard to find elsewhere.

Now, before we start on the first time period, let us go over the basics of genealogical research . . . where to look for information, what to use in your search, and what types of information to look for. Even if you are familiar with "the basics," you still might want to look through this chapter because it points out some of the specialties (relative to general genealogy) that Acadian-Cajun research entails.

TABLE I
ACADIAN-CAJUN SURNAMES

Listed below are 101 surnames that are considered Acadian or Cajun. The Acadian names are those of the French settlers who settled in Acadia in the seventeenth century. The Cajun names also include French, French-Canadian, German, Spanish, and English surnames that joined with the Acadians in the eighteenth century.

NAME	ORIGIN	NAME	ORIGIN
ABSHIRE	G	HEBERT	A
AGUILLARD	SP	HENRY	G
AMY	F	HERNANDEZ	SP
ANDREPONT	F	HERPIN	F
ARCENEAUX	A, C, F	HOLLIER	F
ARDOIN	C	HYMEL	G
AUCOIN	A	JARREAU	F
AUGER	F	JEANSONNE	A, E
AUTHEMENT	F	JOUBERT	F
AUZENNE	F	JUNEAU	C
BABIN	A	LABAUVE	A
BABINEAUX	A	LACOUR	F
BARRAS	F	LAFLEUR	F
BAUDOIN	F	LAFITTE	F
BEGNAUD	F	LALONDE	C
BELLARD	F	LAMBERT	F
BENOIT	A, F	LANDRY	A
BERGERON	A, C	LAVERGNE	F
BERNARD	A, F, S	LEBLANC	A, F
BERTHELOT	F	LEBOEUF	C
BERTRAND	A, C, F, S	LEDET	F
BLANCHARD	A, NE	LEJEUNE	A, C
BONIN	F	LEMOINE	A, F
BONVILLAIN	F	LIRETTE	F
BORDELON	F	LOPEZ	SP
BOREL	E	LOUVIERE	A, C
BOUDREAUX	A	MARCANTEL	I
BOULET	C	MARCEL	F

BOURG	A	MARTIN	A, E, F, SP
BOURGEOIS	A, F	MATHERNE	G
BOUTTE	F	MATTE	C
BRASSEAUX	A	MAYEAUX	F
BREAUX	A	MELANCON	A
BRIGNIC	F	MENARD	F
BROUSSARD	A	MIGUEZ	SP
BRUNET	C	MICHEL	A, F
BURAS	F	MIRE	A
CALLAIS	C	MOREAU	F
CARLIN	I	MORIN	C
CARMOUCHE	F	MOUTON	A
CARRIERE	C	NAQUIN	A
CASTILLE	SP	NUNEZ	SP
CHAMPAGNE	C	OLIVIER	F
CHATAGNIER	F	ORTEGO	SP
CHAUVIN	C	OUBRE	G
CHERAMI	F	OZENNE	F
CHIASSON	A	PATIN	F
CLOUATRE	A	PELLEGRIN	F
COMEAUX	A	PELLERIN	A, F
CORMIER	A	PELLETIER	F
CREDEUR	E	PITRE	A
CROCHET	F	POCHE	G
DAIGLE	A, C	POIRIER	A
DARTES	F	POTIER	A
DECOUX	F, C	PREJEAN	A
DEROUEN	F	PREVOST	F
DESORMEAUX	F	PRIMEAU	F
DESHOTELS	C	PRINCE	A
DESMARETS	F	PRUHDOMME	F, G
DOGUET	C	QUEBEDEAUX	SP
DOIRON	A	RABALAIS	F
DOMINGUE	SP	RACHAL	F
DORE	F	RACHAL	F
DOUCET	A, C	RANSONNET	F
DUBOIS	A, F	RICHARD	A
DUCOTE	C	ROBICHAUX	A
DUFRENE	C	ROBIN	F

DUGAS	A	RODRIGUE	C
DUHON	A	ROGER	A
DUPLECHIN	C, F	ROMAN	F
DUPRE	C	ROMERO	SP
DUPUIS	A, F	ROUSSEL	F
FALCON	SP	ROY	A, C
FALGOUT	F	SAUCIER	F
FERNANDEZ	SP	SAVOY	A
FONTENOT	F	SEGURA	SP
FORET	A	SCHEXNAYDER	G
FRANCOIS	F	SEMER	A
FRIEDRICH	G	SIMON	F
FRUGE	F	SOILEAU	F
FUSELIER	F	SONNIER	A
GAUDET	A	SYLVESTRE	G
GAUDIN	A	THERIOT	A, C
GAUTHIER	F	THIBODEAUX	A, C
GAUTREAUX	A	TOUCHET	G
GIROUARD	A	TOUPS	G
GONSOULIN	F	TRAHAN	A
GRANGER	A, E	TREGRE	G
GRAVOIS	A	VIELLON	F
GREMILLION	F	VERRET	C, F
GUIDRY	A	VIDRINE	F
GUILBEAU	A	VINCENT	A
GUILLORY	F	VOORHIES	D
GUILLOT	A, F	WAGUESPACK	G
HAYDEL	G	WEBRE	G

KEY to ORIGINS

A—Acadia	G—Germany
C—Canada	NE—New England
E—England	S—Switzerland
F—France	SP—Spain / Canary Islands
I—Italian	D—Dutch

II

GENEALOGICAL RESEARCH

GENEALOGY BASICS

Genealogy is the study of your relatives . . . past, present, and future. Relatives of the past are called ancestors and relatives of the future are called descendents. Most people get started in genealogy by trying to determine their direct ancestors (their parents, their grandparents, and so on). You may then move on to research other relatives (past and present) who are not direct ancestors. These are called collateral relatives. Aunts, uncles, and cousins are collateral relatives. You may also want to research all of the descendents of one ancestor. Eventually you may move on to researching lineages other than your own (e.g. your spouse's), just for the enjoyment of "solving the mysteries."

Genealogical research is primarily concerned with four types of information: names, dates, places, and relationships. The trick is to fit them all together so that they make up your correct lineage.

NAMES

You will be looking for surnames (last names) and given names. They are the basic link with the past. When writing surnames, you will find it beneficial to put them in all capital letters (e.g. Jean Baptiste HEBERT). You will often find them written this way in resource books. This helps you to distinguish surnames from the rest of the text.

Watch out for "*dit*" names (e.g. Jean THERIOT *dit* LEROUX). It was not uncommon for people to take on other surnames. They may have done this for a number of reasons . . . someone by that name helped raise them, they admired someone by that name, they were descriptive nicknames and so on. Etienne BREAUX *dit* CORMIER may have had a father named BREAUX, but was brought up by someone named CORMIER. His children may take the name BREAUX, CORMIER, or BREAUX *dit* CORMIER!

You will need to be able to interpret abbreviations of names. Usually this can be done by using common sense. Some examples are: Jos.=Joseph, Bte.=Baptiste, and Wm.=William.

9

Women are almost always referred to by their maiden names. If your ancestor Marie PITRE married a Jean BLANCHARD, you would look for her name under PITRE in indexes and in records. This can be very helpful in your search. Suppose you were looking for a couple, Jean HEBERT and his wife, Maria BOUDREAUX. There might be two or more Jean HEBERTs with wives named Maria. The wife's maiden name helps you pinpoint the correct one. Also, having maiden names helps to determine the parents of female ancestors.

The given names (first and middle) have only the first letter capitalized. Be sure to include all of the names that you find and in all of their variations. Watch for juxtaposition of the first and middle names. Your great-grandfather Jacques may have Pierre Jacques for his given name. It was common (up to the early part of this century) to call someone by their middle name. So, if you know a record for Jacques should exist in a certain place but cannot find it, look for someone with Jacques for a middle name.

Names are often found misspelled. When you have an English-speaking census-taker writing down the French name of an Acadian person, you are apt to get just about anything. Even today, many people outside Louisiana misspell names like LeBOEUF and HEBERT. Names were often spelled phonetically. HEBERT might turn into EBAIR, ABARE, or HEBAIRE. Sometimes names were translated into other language equivalents; Pierre would become Pedro, Etienne would become Steven, LEBLANC would become WHITE, and so on. With the variety of nationalities in early Louisiana, it was quite common for the names being written to be a foreign language to the writer. Some names may have over a dozen variations. Be sure to write down what you find exactly as you find it. Do not make assumptions until you have other evidence. For example, if you find someone called GAUDI, do not just assume that the name is GAUDET and copy it as such. It may actually be GODIN. If you make an incorrect assumption, you could easily wind up down the wrong path.

Abetting the name problem is the high illiteracy rate before this century. Literacy was not the highest priority in the past. Many people could not even spell their own names. So, they were of no help when someone would write their names (or dates, places, etc.) incorrectly. On official documents (e.g. marriage licenses), the preparer would sign the names and the people would just mark an "X" between their first and last names. This continued even into the early twentieth century.

DATES

You will be looking for three major dates for each person: birth, marriage, and death. Birth and marriage dates will be easier to find because the Catholic church kept better records of these. Death (funeral) records were less frequently recorded. An exact date (date, month, and year) is best, although you will often be dealing with approximations. The international form for writing dates in genealogy is date, month, and year (e.g. 21 SEP 1961). If you insist on using a different format, just be sure to keep it uniform in all of your records. You would not want May 11 written as 5/11 to be interpreted as November 5.

If you find two dates for an event, write both of them down . . . especially if neither is a primary source. You can hopefully pinpoint the exact date later on. Learn how to approximate dates. If someone is 42 in the 1870 census, then he was born about 1828 (1870-42=1828). Be careful, though; censuses, although filled with abundant information, are notorious for incorrect dating. Dates and ages given were often estimated and were often incorrect by months or even years.

PLACES

You will be looking for where each person was born, where they were married, and where they died (and were buried). Other significant places should also be noted if they lived or even visited other locations.

Places are necessary because they not only tell a lot about the location of your past, but they also help to solve puzzles in other areas. Finding the location of a couple's marriage may help in finding the birthplace (and corresponding records) of their children. If you do not know places, your search could be much harder, too. Knowing that a certain relative lived in Lafourche Parish in 1870 means you only have to search that parish in the 1870 census.

Without that knowledge, you might have to search through several parishes looking for that person.

Be aware that place names do change. Since parish, state, and territory lines have changed in the past, it is important to know where they were for the time period you are researching. If someone was in the southern part of Lafayette Parish in the 1840 census, you will need to look in Vermilion Parish in the 1850 census because Vermilion was part of Lafayette Parish in 1840. Consult maps of Louisiana parish locations at the time the census was taken.

RELATIONSHIPS

Finding how and to whom you are related is the basic goal of this research. Many of your ancestors' names, dates, and places are already in books (and other reference material), but you do not know how they relate to you. Sometimes relationships are given and sometimes you have to figure them out. For example, some marriage licenses may give relationships (Jean HEBERT, son of Pierre and Suzanne PITRE). It helps a great deal when a relationship is given and not just the name. Other records may just give the name (e.g. Pierre HEBERT's name as just a witness to Jean HEBERT's wedding is not nearly as useful).

Sometimes it must be done in a backdoor fashion by looking at the records of other relatives (direct and collateral). For example, a birth record for a sibling or cousin may identify the maternal and/or paternal grandparents names that you need in your line. This could validate a relationship that was not listed elsewhere. Establishing relationships is done through careful examination of the names, dates, places, and relationships you find. Once all of the research is done, you will know how you are related to the hundreds of people you have found.

WHERE TO GO

One of the first things you need to know when researching your ancestors is where to look for information. All of the material you need to unpuzzle your ancestry is useless if you cannot find it. The most common places to look are your family and personal documents, libraries, courthouses, churches, and cemeteries.

FAMILY & PERSONAL DOCUMENTATION

Step number one . . . ask Mom and Dad (if they are still around). Then move on to grandparents, aunts, uncles, and so on. Be sure to ask if anyone in the family has already worked on your family's ancestry. Even if it is only a cousin, you can still use much of the material. Look through your family's personal documents . . . Bibles, marriage licenses, etc. If your relatives are scattered about, you may want to conduct parts of this research by phone or mail.

LIBRARIES

Once you have queried your relatives and examined family documentation, you have to look to outside sources. The first place most people go to is the library. Libraries hold the most information for a genealogist. They contain censuses, newspapers, church records, family genealogies, and genealogical periodicals. It is often unnecessary to dig around cemeteries or search through volumes of courthouse and church records. Much of the material relevant to us as genealogists has been transcribed and published in books or periodicals. The Appendix contains a listing of the best Acadian-Cajun libraries.

As you may expect, most genealogical information on Acadians and Cajuns is in Louisiana and Canadian libraries. Check with the libraries to see if they publish a list of their genealogical holdings. The Bayouland Library System (a collection of the parish libraries in south central Louisiana), for example, publishes a *Bayouland Genealogical Resources Catalog* that lists the publications in its libraries and where they are found. More information on this publication, last revised in 1985 and selling for $15.00, can be obtained from The Bayouland Library System, 301 W. Congress, Lafayette, LA 70501. A supplement was published in 1992.

If there is a "main" Acadian library in Louisiana, it would have to be the Dupré Library at USL in Lafayette. Dupré Library houses the Center for Louisiana Studies, which is emerging as *the* repository for Acadian-Cajun material, just as the Centre d'Etudes Acadiennes (see below) is the Acadian center for Canada (and the world).

There is also a bit more than usual at libraries in the Northeast (e.g. Maine) and St. Louis, Missouri, since quite a few Acadian and Cajun ancestors passed through and settled in those places. If you live elsewhere in the country, your local library may not have much Acadian-Cajun information. But it is possible for you to take advantage of the Acadian-Cajun libraries without traveling to them on your own.

Interlibrary loans allow you to have books and microfilm sent from those libraries to your local library. Of course, some genealogical material is not loaned out, but much is available. Check with your local library for details on how the interlibrary loan system works. It may be your only way of doing the proper research if you cannot go personally to the materials.

If you are familiar with computers, you might be able to make use of some type of in-home library. There are a number of on-line card catalogs and document-retrieval systems that can be accessed by computer modem.

Also, microfilm is available from private sources and the National Archives. The American Genealogical Lending Library (AGLL) is a private company that rents microfilm of passenger lists, all U.S. censuses, military records, and other topics for about $3 a roll. Microfilm can be purchased for less than $15 a roll. A yearly membership fee of $30 gets you a large catalog of their holdings and two free rentals. AGLL does not have "Acadian" or "Cajun" material as such, but the censuses, passenger lists, etc. can be helpful if you do not have local access to them.

Archives contain material similar to that found in libraries. The National Archives (Washington, D.C. 20408) contains a wealth of information available on microfilm (which can be rented or purchased). Its censuses and military records are a most useful item that they have relevant to the Acadian-Cajun researcher. A book is available (*The Archives*) detailing the Archives' holdings at the six regional branch divisions. Check with your local library (or write to the Archives directly) for other publications on the Archives' holdings, and do not forget state and provincial archives.

The Louisiana Archives contain much of the available south Louisiana and Cajun material. They also have a most helpful staff. Canadian archives (national and provincial) contain much of the available Acadian material, though it is harder to access from the United States. Archives are particularly good sources for census information, military records, and passenger lists.

The Mormon Church Library (based in Salt Lake City, but with over 1000 branches around the country) contains an abundant amount of genealogical material. Genealogy is an integral part of the Mormon religion. They have collected millions upon millions of records from around the world. Their branch libraries can get microfilms and microfiche on loan from their main library for you to use (on the premises only). A book is available (*The Library*) that gives details on what is available. The branch libraries have detailed catalogs of everything that can be ordered. Check with your local Mormon church for the location of the nearest branch library.

The Library of Congress, of course, has just about any book you could ask for. A book has been written (*The Library of Congress*) that will descibe what is there.

The Centre D'Etudes Acadiennes at the University of Moncton (in Moncton, New Brunswick) has the world's largest collection of Acadian material. It has almost 10,000 works related to the Acadians. A three volume set (*Inventaire des Sources Documentaires sur les Acadiens*) has been published by the Centre that lists their materials.

Regional libraries around the Maritimes tend to emphasize English history (since the English have been "in charge" since 1713), but the early Acadian material can still be found. The library at Université Sainte-Anne's (Church Point, Nova Scotia) contains a good bit of material. And they have a room that has a wall covered with the coats of arms of Acadian families.

COURTHOUSES

Courthouses are another domain of genealogists. Courthouses may contain a number of valuable primary documents that can help you with genealogy. These records include marriage licenses, original acts, conveyances, successions, wills, probates, civil suits, naturalization records, land records, and other miscellaneous civil records (e.g. power of attorney). When visiting an unfamiliar courthouse, it is best to ask what types of information they have. Usually, all of these records are in the courthouse. But sometimes they are located elsewhere. For example, many of the old records for Lafourche Parish are located in the old parish jail.

Marriage licenses are available back to the 1700s (depending upon the parish). Remember that the date on the license is often not the date of the marriage. The wedding could have been days, weeks, or even months away. The church record of the marriage has the exact date. Marriage licenses often give the parents' names.

Conveyances and original acts contain a variety of document forms. They primarily involve sales and purchases of land, but may also include civil suits and other legal transactions. Some of the early records are in French. Fortunately, many courthouses have translated the French documents into English.

Successions, wills, and probates relate to the estate of an individual. There may or may not be records of this type pertaining to your ancestor. Often one or more of these documents will exist if the ancestor was wealthy or there was a problem with the estate (e.g. he owed considerable money when he died).

Civil suits are the lawsuits arising from disputes between private citizens. Some of these are useless, but others do contain useful genealogical information. Civil suits are indexed twice . . . under the names of the defendant and the plaintiff. Be sure to look in both indexes.

The land records are of several forms. Records of the land concessions to the original settlers may be found. Some courthouses have a set of the *American State Papers*. These books detail the land records of the early 1800s, when the United States was deciding who owned what land. There are several other books (that list various land transactions) that will appear in later chapters that are available in libraries. Tract and plat maps are available at parish courthouses (and at the Louisiana State Land Office) that date back to the mid-1800s.

Remember that land records (sales, purchases, disputes) can also be found in conveyances and original acts. These may be useful in that a record may mention heirs to a piece of land or it may tell that the land once belonged to the father (and give his name). They may also help to verify an identity.

There are an assortment of other records, including power of attorney, bonds, corporations, mortgages, inquests, etc. These usually are not helpful; but if you are really stuck on someone they may be worth a try. If they are indexed, it should not take too long to review them.

In some cases, courthouse records may have been transcribed and printed in a book or periodical. We will cover the published material (in book form) in this book at the appropriate point. Many early acts have been published in book form. Many other records have been in genealogical periodicals. Check the *Acadian-Cajun Genealogical Periodical Article Index* to see if what you need is in a periodical. This book, compiled by Timothy Hebert, lists over 5,000 articles in over twenty periodicals relating to Acadian-Cajun genealogy. It is available from the author (P.O. Box 1416, Houma, LA 70361). If the records have not been previously printed, you will need to go to the courthouse itself. And just because it *has* been printed, do not rule out going to the courthouse. Sometimes transcribed materials contain errors or do not mention everything in the document.

Most courthouses have indexes to each type of record, so your task is not as hard as it seems. Be aware that some records might have been lost or burned in a fire. Ask the clerk of court if there are any peculiarities for the parish's history, what records are available for that parish, and how the indexes are arranged. And remember, women may be listed by either their maiden or their married surnames, so look under both.

Table II below lists the location of courthouses in Louisiana and when each parish was founded. Note that if an ancestor lived in a parish before it was formed, you will need to look in the records of the original parish from which it was formed. For example, courthouse records for an ancestor who lived in the Lafayette area around 1810 would be found in the St. Martin Parish courthouse. Canada (Acadia) is not included, because the Acadians didn't have courthouses back then.

You can usually get courthouse offices to make copies of documents; but be aware that it costs much more than the library's photocopy machine. Courthouse offices may charge up to one dollar each for copies. So, if you need quite a few copies, you may need to stop by the bank first. If the information is brief, or if you do not need an actual photocopy, you will save a lot of money by just copying what you need from the records. Please remember to write down where you found the information.

If you are not good at reading handwritten script, you had better start practicing. Most pre-twentieth-century documents were handwritten, and the legibility varies. Some documents may take a while to "decipher." Some documents may also be in a foreign language (usually French or Spanish). If no translation has been done, you can either plow through it word by word with a dictionary or have someone translate it for you. Computer software has recently been produced that can translate foreign language material into English. One of the most popular is Language Assistant by Microtac Software. Contact Selective Software (1-800-423-3556) or Microtac (1-619-272-5700) for more information on these programs.

One last point . . . please be careful. In some cases you will be handling original documents over 100 years old! Please handle them carefully so that they will be around for the next generation of genealogists. You are handling pieces of history. Some people, unfortunately, try to bring home original documents as "souvenirs." Needless to say, this is a crime. A photocopy or transcription will have the information you need. Please return the originals to the same place in

TABLE II
ACADIANA AREA COURTHOUSES

PARISH	CREATED	FORMED FROM	PARISH SEAT	ZIP CODE
Acadia	1886	St. Landry	Crowley	70526
Ascension	1807	Original	Donaldsonville	70346
Assumption	1807	Original	Napoleonville	70390
Avoyelles	1807	Original	Marksville	71351
Calcasieu	1840	St. Landry	Lake Charles	70601
Cameron	1870	Calcasieu	Cameron	70631
East Baton Rouge	1810	Original	Baton Rouge	70801
Evangeline	1911	St. Landry	Ville Platte	70586
Iberia	1868	St. Martin/ St. Mary	New Iberia	70560
Iberville	1807	Original	Plaquemine	70764
Jefferson Davis	1913	Calcasieu	Jennings	70546
Lafayette	1823	St. Martin	Lafayette	70501
Lafourche	1807	Original	Thibodaux	79301
Orleans	1807	Original	New Orleans	70112
Plaquemines	1807	Orleans	Pointe à la Hache	70082
Pointe Coupee	1807	Original	New Roads	70760
St. Bernard	1807	Orleans	Chalmette	70043
St. Charles	1807	Original	Hahnville	70057
St. James	1807	Original	Convent	70723
St. John/Baptist	1807	Original	Edgard	70049
St. Landry	1807	Original	Opelousas	70570
St. Martin	1807	Original	St. Martinville	70582
St. Mary	1811	Attakapas	Franklin	70538
Terrebonne	1822	Lafourche	Houma	70360
Vermilion	1844	Lafayette	Abbeville	70510
West Baton Rouge	1807	Original	Port Allen	70767

For records in a parish before it was formed, look in the parish from which it was taken. Louisiana was divided into 19 parishes in 1807. Later on, new parishes were formed from parts of the original parishes. The published 1810 census of Louisiana has a section prepared on the exact movement of parish lines through the years.

which they were found. Just think how you would feel if someone had misplaced a record you desperately need. If you would like to have a replica to frame, have the photocopy reproduced on parchment paper. For the sake of future generations and history, do not bring home any "souvenirs" except those that come out of a photocopier!

CHURCHES

Church records are a valuable source for any genealogist. As previously mentioned, the Acadian-Cajun genealogist is quite fortunate that almost all Acadians and Cajuns before the twentieth century were Catholic. Their church records were reasonably well kept and abstracts of most pre-1900 records have been published.

Other religions record vital statistics (births, marriages, deaths/funerals), but none as thoroughly as the Catholics. Also, most of the old records are kept in district diocese archives. You do not have to hop from town to town to get records from several churches. In addition to all of this, most of the Catholic church records of south Louisiana for the eighteenth and nineteenth centuries have been transcribed and published. Rev. Donald Hebert's *Southwest Louisiana Records* lists church (and some civil) records for southwest Louisiana up to the twentieth century. His series on *South Louisiana Records* (Terrebonne and Lafourche parishes) does likewise. The Baton Rouge Diocese has published thirteen volumes (to date) of their records (to the year 1876). The Archdiocese of New Orleans has published seven volumes (to the year 1803). So, there is no need to spend hours scrutinizing French and Spanish documents; it has already been done for you. Chapter 4 has details on what these records entail and how to understand them.

This book will only cover Catholic church records, since most Acadians and Cajuns were Catholic. Protestant religions did not really make much of an impact until the later part of the nineteenth century and in the twentieth century. Unlike the Catholic church, there are no central archives for Protestant records. You will most probably have to go to the church to find records (if they still exist).

Rev. Donald Hebert's *Guide to Church Records in Louisiana, 1720-1975* lists Catholic as well as Protestant churches in Louisiana. A description of the original church records can be found in *A Southern Catholic Heritage* (Nolan). The book also gives a brief history of the early Catholic churches in Louisiana.

The church records contain births (and/or baptisms), marriages, and deaths (usually in the form of funeral dates). Parents for those involved in the event are often given. Other information (godparents, previous spouses, ages, etc.) may also be found from time to time. For example, ecclesiastical marriage records may also provide information about the groom's birthplace. Churches and church archives can also provide you with an extraction or copy of a record. The method and cost vary from place to place. Some let you search for yourself, while others can only be accessed through correspondence. Table III gives the Catholic dioceses of Louisiana and pertinent data on each.

TABLE III
DIOCESES OF LOUISIANA - ARCHIVES

Archdiocese of New Orleans   (504) 529-2651
    1100 Chartres
    New Orleans, LA 70116-2596
    Erected 1793
    Includes the parishes of: St. Charles, St. John the Baptist,
        Jefferson, Washington, St. Tammany,
        St. Bernard, Plaquemines, and Orleans

Diocese of Baton Rouge   (504) 387-0561
    1800 S. Acadian Thruway
    P.O. Box 2028
    Baton Rouge, LA 70821
    Erected 1961
    Includes the parishes of: Pointe Coupee, Iberville,
        Assumption, St. James, Ascension, East & West
        Baton Rouge, East & West Feliciana, St. Helena,
        Livingston, and Tangipagoa

Diocese of Lafayette   (318) 261-5639
    Diocesan Office Building
    1408 Carmel Ave.
    P.O. Box 3387

Lafayette, LA 70501
Erected 1918
Includes the civil parishes of: Acadia, Evangeline,
 Vermilion, St. Landry, Lafayette, St. Martin,
 Iberia, and most of St. Mary

Diocese of Houma-Thibodaux   (504) 446-2383
205 Audubon Avenue
Thibodaux, LA 70301
Erected 1977
Includes the parishes of: Terrebonne, Lafourche, some of St.
 Mary, and Grand Isle
The Archives are located on the Nicholls State
 University campus in Thibodaux.

Diocese of Alexandria   (318) 445-2401
4400 Coliseum Blvd.
P.O. Box 7417
Alexandria, LA 71306
Erected 1853
Includes the central Louisiana parishes

Diocese of Shreveport   (318) 222-2006
2500 Line Ave.
Shreveport, LA 71104-3043
Erected 1986
Includes the northern Louisiana parishes

CEMETERIES

Cemeteries may be one of the least used resources for research. The library is a much more comfortable place to work (and there are not nearly as many dead bodies there). Cemeteries do contain valuable genealogical data, and you cannot afford to overlook them. In some cases, cemetery field work is not necessary. Many cemeteries have had the lists of their "occupants" transcribed and published. The WPA did cemetery listings for some Louisiana parishes years ago. There are also recent books with cemetery listings (see the Appendix), as well as cemetery listings in periodicals (consult the *Acadian-Cajun Genealogical Periodical Article Index*). If you cannot find a list for the cemetery in question, you may just have to hit the old tombstone trail. It can be quite an interesting experience. Discovering the gravesite of your great-great grandfather gives you a certain feeling that's hard to describe.

Cemeteries are not the ideal sources of information, however. Sometimes they are inconvenient to search. Often the tombstones are so weathered that they are illegible. You will not find much information on people who died over one hundred years ago. They usually did not have sturdy headstones on graves back then; and if they did, weathering and other types of damage have had a better chance to take their toll. The earliest gravesites usually date back to the early 1800s (and there are not many).

OTHER PLACES

Of course, there are other places to find data, but they may be harder to get to or harder to understand. Some types of records (local and international) are difficult to get to; some of these records have been published and some have not. There are Acadian records in France and Spain, but most people do not travel to Europe that often. You may write to specific places in France (or Germany, Switzerland, etc. for Cajun ancestors' material), but it is much harder to do research by international mail to someone in a foreign language. Some libraries (e.g. Morman Genealogical Library) have copies of many international records. You might want to try them first, before you schedule an international jaunt or try a correspondence campaign. Fortunately, if you've reached the point where you must consult these sources, you probably have quite a bit done on your ancestry. So you will be better exposed to difficult genealogical research techniques.

Some sources of information are hard to understand. In some cases, learning how to extract the information or trying to understand what you find may not be worth the effort. New Orleans has many notarial acts stored in the Notarial Archives, but most of them are not transcribed. The Black Box records from the eighteenth century are also in New Orleans. How are you at reading 200-year-old handwritten French and Spanish? Most people have trouble trying to read French or Spanish in modern type!

As previously mentioned, this book will not give you an advanced course in genealogical technique. If you use just the sources listed here, you should be able to complete most of your ancestry. By that time, you will have been exposed to enough of the advanced techniques that you will know where to go to learn more (and to break through those "brick wall" ancestors).

Some of you at this point are saying, "Great! There are tons of material on Acadians and Cajuns . . . but I live hundreds of miles away! How can I get to this wealth of genealogical data?" Interlibrary loans and microfilm rentals are your best bet, but that takes time, some things still are not in print (or on microfilm) and some materials cannot be loaned out.

If you cannot get to the information and it cannot be sent to your library, the next step is correspondence. If you do not like to write letters, you're in for some bad news. Genealogists usually end up writing a lot to get information from elsewhere.

But to whom do I write? Look at Acadian-Cajun genealogical periodicals for someone working on the same material you are. You might be able to find some of these periodicals at your local library. The best thing to do is to join one or more of the genealogical societies located in your search areas. These societies encompass local, regional, state, and national areas. A listing of Louisiana and Canadian genealogical societies with Acadian-Cajun ties can be found in the Appendix. The annual cost is usually $20 or less and includes a one year subscription to their periodical. Once you get a copy of their publication, look at the Query section. This is where people who have run into the proverbial brick wall ask for help. And this is where you can put your inquiry. Chances are, if it's not an ancestor who's got everybody stuck, you will get one (or more) answers to your request. You may find people mentioned in these periodicals that you could write to for information. If you live close enough, try to attend the society meetings and seminars. You will meet other genealogists that might have just what you need. A fellow amateur genealogist may save you hours of research when you find that they've already done the work themselves.

As you get further involved with your genealogical project, you will probably be writing to individuals . . . other genealogists working on common ancestors, clerks of court for copies of marriage licenses, and so on. A basic genealogical form letter is available from Everton or Genealogy Unlimited (see the Appendix). And *please* remember to always include return postage. A self-addressed stamped envelope is even better. Some people receive quite a bit a mail, and they do not want to have to foot the bill in addition to helping everyone out.

PROFESSIONAL GENEALOGISTS

If something has got you completely lost, or if you'd just rather pay someone to do all of the legwork, people are available to help you. Some genealogists, professional and amateur, will work for others for a fee. The cost varies and results cannot be guaranteed, but it may be your only choice. Professional genealogists charge by the hour ($5 on up) and usually require a minimum number of hours. You may want to write to a genealogical society in the area in which you are interested for help in contacting a genealogist to help you.

You may also find someone in an ad in *The Genealogical Helper*. It is a national publication available around the country. (I'd recommend you get at least one copy of this magazine so that you will know what is out there in the field of genealogy.] Genealogists often advertise their services in the magazine. Some of them may specialize in Louisiana or Canadian researching.

There are also specialized searchers who will search a particular type of records for you. For example, SBL Enterprises (Box 261, Lancaster, TX 75146) will conduct searches of Civil War records and books. Others will search census records for a fee. This can be extremely helpful if you do not have access to censuses or do not have the time to search them. Be aware that each name variation calls for a separate search. So if a name has two variations, it may require two separate searches.

A listing of all Certified Genealogists can be purchased for $2 from the Board for Certification of Genealogists, P.O. Box 19165, Washington, D.C., 20036-01655.

MATERIALS AND EQUIPMENT

The basic materials for genealogy can be quite simple . . . paper and pencil. You can get much of the work done by just collecting the information on loose-leaf paper and drawing up your own ancestry chart. Of course, it can get more complicated; but it doesn't have to get very expensive. You may want to carry a set of 3x5 cards in a card file to jot down information. A tape recorder can be helpful to get information, although libraries may object if you talk too loud.

You will start out using charts and forms to compile the data. You may want to then put the information on a computer to manipulate it easier. You **will** be using photocopy machines and microfilm readers, but they are quite simple to operate. Let's start out with the basic tools.

CHARTS

There are a number of different charts and forms available to make your task easier. The two major types (of which several variations exist) are the pedigree chart and the family group chart. Pedigree charts give a graphical representation of one person and that person's direct ancestors (parents, grandparents, etc.) for three to six generations. There is usually space for jotting down vital statistics (birth, marriage, death). The people are numbered with the Ahnentafel numbering system.

> **The Ahnentafel numbering system** assigns each person a number that relates to his/her ancestors and descendants. You double a person's number to get the father's number. You double a person's number and add one to get the mother's number. Looking at it the other way, a child's number is one half of the father's number and one half of [the mother's number minus one]. Let's look at an example for a fictitious Jean BREAUX. His Ahnentafel number is 24. His father's number would be 48 (2x24) and his mother's would be 49 (2x24+1). His wife's number would be 25 (24+1). His children's number would be 12 (24/2). Notice that there is only one possible number for the child. This numbering system is only useful for direct ancestry and runs into problems if you want to include collateral realtives (e.g. siblings).

```
                                          4 Jean's father's father
                         2 Jean's father  |
                         |                5 Jean's father's mother
1 Jean BREAUX  |
                         |                6 Jean's mother's father
                         3 Jean's mother  |
                                          7 Jean's mother's mother
```

The usual pedigree chart gives the basic Ahnentafel numbers of 1-31 (5 gen. chart) or 1-15 (4 gen. chart). The problem is, once you get past the first sheet, the numbers do not relate back to the first person on chart #1 (usually you). So, on our chart (see the Appendix), you have a space to put in the correct Ahnentafel number that relates to the very first person on the first chart (YOU).

The most common chart is the five generation chart. The pedigree chart printed in the Appendix is a four generation chart that was specifically designed for this book. The normal five generation chart gives you barely enough room for basic data and no room to write down references. As we will see later, keeping track of your sources . . . where you get the information . . . is **extremely important**. Our four generation chart has space for you to write down the references. Yes, you're supposed to write down the references on the family group charts, but you will inevitably find yourself working from just the pedigree chart at times. So now you have no excuse for not jotting down the sources. The charts in the appendix may be copied and enlarged on a photocopier (for your personal use only . . . **not for resale**). Full size charts can also be ordered from the author (P.O. Box 1416, Houma, LA 70361) for $5.00 per 100.

Pedigree charts are also found in two orientations . . . vertical and horizontal. Our pedigree chart is vertical, because we find it easier to handle the pages if they're in a standard book format. Using horizontal charts can sometimes be awkward. If, however, you feel more comfortable with a five generation chart and/or a horizontal format chart, they are available from any genealogical supply company (see the Appendix).

The other major chart type is the family group chart. Again, there are several variations to be found. The chart in the Appendix is our own version. Unlike other charts, it allows room for Ahnentafel numbers and sources. You should make out one chart for every married couple. Be sure to note the references. If you have a reference or note on a child that doesn't have his own chart, you should footnote it at the bottom of the page. Keeping track of all children is important if you later want to do work on collateral relatives.

You can also purchase large charts (legal size on up to wall size) on which to place more than four or five generations. It can be helpful to put your information on one big chart so that you can visualize what material you have and what material you need to work on.

There are other types of charts that help in specialized areas. There are census charts for the years 1810-1920. Even though the United States had censuses in 1790 and 1800, there was none done for Louisiana since the United States did not aquire the Louisiana Territory until 1803. Most of the censuses have different pieces of information. Each of these forms allows you to keep track of the information you extract from the censuses without confusion. There is also a form for recording census information for one family line through all of the censuses. A good selection of census forms is available from Everton or Genealogy Unlimited (see Appendix) for five cents apiece.

You may have realized that you will soon have accumulated quite a number of papers. The best way to handle this is to keep them in a three-ring binder. These binders and the three-hole punchers are readily available, and they allow you to add or remove papers easily. You should also use folders and a filing cabinet to organize the multitude of papers that you will accumulate.

COMPUTERS

Of course, the easiest way to handle all of this information would be with a computer. The most popular computer today is the IBM compatible (MS-DOS) computer. There are several programs available for this computer, ranging from simple programs for less than $5 to detailed, comprehensive programs for several hundred dollars. There are also several programs available for Apple and Commodore computers. The essential components for genealogical purposes are the computer/monitor, printer, and disk drive (preferably a hard drive). This book will not try to explain how to use a computer, but it will concentrate on the use of one for genealogical purposes.

IBM compatibles can use the widest variety of software. Several shareware programs are available for less than $5 (see the Appendix for vendors' names and addresses). These programs allow you to store your data and print it out. As you move up in price, you get more features. The three major programs in use are Family Roots, Roots III, and PAF.

Family Roots is distributed by Quinsoft (1-800-637-7668) and sells for $225. Formats are available for IBM compatibles, Apple, Commodore 64, TRS-80, and Macintosh. Roots III is distributed by Commsoft (1-800-327-6687) and sells for $259. It is designed for IBM compatibles. Commsoft also has several "accessory" programs that work with Roots III. Roots III is probably your best bet if you ultimately want to put your work into print. The best buy of all has to be PAF (Personal Ancestral File). This program, distributed by the Mormon Church (801-531-2584), sells for just $35. It lacks some of the bells and whistles of the other two, but it does a good job for a very affordable price. Other programs are also available. Check out the ads in a copy of *The Genealogical Helper*, which is available at libraries throughout the country. The more expensive programs are often available at discounts.

If you do not have a computer and do not want to (or cannot) get one, do not worry. The computer makes things easier and manipulates data faster, but you can still complete your genealogical research without even going near a computer.

MICROFILM READERS/PRINTERS

It shouldn't be too long after starting your research before you are faced with using microfilm. Microfilm (and microfiche) is being used more and more because of its compactness and ease in reproduction.

There are several types of microfilm reader/printers. The old ones have only one lens, use thermal paper, and have to be advanced by a hand crank. The newest ones have motorized advance/rewind, use plain paper, and a zoom lens (to enlarge or reduce an image). There are a number of machines in between these two types with an assortment of features. If you have any doubts about using them, just ask the librarian for help. Some even have the directions printed on the machine. Some microfilm readers also have a printer built into them.

Microfilm reader/printers allow you to make a copy of what you are viewing. These copies may be a positive image (black print comes out black) or a negative image (black -> white, white -> black). The newer ones usually make positive images. You may have to make a test print to make sure the exposure is set correctly. It is best to ask for help from the librarian the first time you work a microfilm printer. Microfilm prints usually cost ten to twenty-five cents, although some places charge up to one dollar. They are usually not coin-operated. Once you make the copies, you must go to the desk to pay for them.

Microfiche is a small sheet of film that contains a number of pages greatly reduced. A special viewer (or viewer/printer) is available to use. There is not a great deal of Acadian-Cajun material on microfiche. Check with the Mormon library, Everton Publishers, and AGLL for their holdings.

PHOTOCOPY MACHINES

Most people have used photocopy machines before. If you haven't, you are about to be introduced to them in a big way. You will be making dozens, if not hundreds, of copies in your research. In some cases, you will want a copy just to have it (e.g. your great-grandparents marriage license), while you usually will use it to get information to apply to your charts.

You may find pages and pages of information while at a library in another city. Photocopying allows you to take the vital information home with you to work on at your leisure. If you try to write down all of the information and apply it to your charts while you are at the library, you'll be there for days instead of hours.

There are several types of photocopy machines. The main features to consider are: what sizes does it make, what is the maximum size that can be copied, can it reduce or enlarge, and how much does it cost. Some copiers can only copy up to a legal size sheet of paper, while others can copy up to 11x17 inches (2 standard size sheets, side-by-side). It is useful to be able to copy up to 11x17 because you can then copy two sheets at once (and divide your cost in half). Copiers usually have at least two trays of paper . . . one standard size (8 1/2x11) and one legal size (8 1/2x14). Some copiers have 11x17 paper; this allows you to copy two sheets of paper side by side without reducing them. Reducing and enlarging are available on the better copiers. This lets you put two pages on one standard or legal sheet if the copier doesn't have 11x17 paper (and most do not). The print is smaller, but it cuts your copying costs in half.

The cost of a copy varies from five to twenty-five cents, though the cost may go up to a dollar at courthouses. Some copiers accept dollar bills, although most are coin-operated. Some places require you to pay at the desk. Otherwise, you have to bring change along with you. Most locations can give you change for currency, but it is best to play it safe. So bring a roll of dimes or quarters with you if you plan to do a lot of copying. You are usually allowed to make the copies yourself, though some places require a staff member to make any copies.

TYPES OF INFORMATION

There are several types of information that you will be dealing with. These include oral testimony, original documentation, books, periodicals, and microfilm.

ORAL TESTIMONY

Oral testimony is when someone tells you the information. This is usually only useful for material on one to four generations back in time. Information told to you by your parents or grandparents would fall into this category. You may want to record this on tape (with the person's permission), or at the very least . . . try to transcribe it as you hear it. This type of information could be vital in getting you started. You may find some conflicting testimony, however. Just write it down, and you can deal with "who's right" later on.

Please treat older relatives carefully. It may take a bit of persistence to get the information you need. This topic will be further pursued in the next chapter.

Oral testimony may also include correspondence and telephone conversations. Sometimes the best and/or only way to communicate with a relative living elsewhere is by mail or telephone.

ORIGINAL DOCUMENTATION

Original documentation includes birth certificates, marriage licenses, family Bibles, church records (at the church), courthouse records, etc. If you can easily get your hands on it, it probably is very recent (within 75 years). This will usually be information that you or your relatives have in your possession. Older documentation exists at churches and courthouses. You can usually go to the proper courthouse and actually see your great-grandparents marriage license. Even if the records have been transcribed or indexed, you may want to view the original papers. It may list things that could help you that were not recorded by the transcriber. Also, the transcriber could have made a mistake.

The term primary documentation is often used in place of original documentation. Primary documentation is that information recorded at the time of the event (e.g. a birth certificate). The next level of documentation is secondary documentation (e.g. newspaper account). Of course, the most desirable type of documentation to find is primary; although you will end up using many secondary sources because the primary sources do not exist, cannot be used, or are difficult to access.

BOOKS

There are several types of books that you will be consulting. Some books are family history books and genealogies that give the ancestors or descendants of one particular person. This could be helpful if you share an ancestor with someone in the book. Some books contain transcriptions of original documentation. These books contain material that would take you months to search out on your own. They include church records, civil records, censuses, passenger lists, and land titles. Some books are just indexes. They index another large work, such as a census.

Most of the books mentioned are indexed in the back of the book. You can just look through the indexes to see if the ancestor in question is covered in that source. Indexes can save you hours of time. Remember to look for alternate spellings. The original writer or the transcriber for the index may have misspelled a name. And remember to look for women under their maiden names.

PERIODICALS

Genealogical periodicals hold a vast amount of information, much of which is not printed in books. It is usually the same type of information found in books, but not lengthy enough to be put in book form. Information on the area you are searching will most likely be found in the genealogical periodical of the society located in that area; although it may be found in a periodical by a neighboring society. The advice given on indexes for books applies to periodicals as well. You may find an ancestor through the index in an article that you would have otherwise ignored. Remember to try and join a genealogical society in the area(s) that you are working on. Membership entitles you to a subscription to their periodical (see the listing in the Appendix). Be aware that long articles may be continued in multiple issues. A long article may be published over several issues. *The Acadian-Cajun Genealogical Periodical Article Index* lists over 5000 articles in 21 Acadian-Cajun, Louisiana, and Canadian genealogical periodicals. If you want to know if a topic has been published in a genealogical periodical, this is the book to consult.

MICROFILM

Materials that are bulky or are not in print can often be found on microfilm. Microfilms are simply photographs taken of printed/written material. A large book can easily fit on one roll of microfilm. You can view the images on a microfilm reader. If you want a copy of a page, you can have it printed out on a microfilm printer. The U.S. censuses are all on microfilm. Newspapers are put on microfilm. Can you imagine the condition of an orginal nineteenth-century newspaper after a number of people have looked through it? Microfilm allows you to see the material without damaging the originals. Be careful how you handle the microfilm, though, because it can be scratched. There are quite a few other sources on microfilm, such as civil records, land records, military records, etc. Smaller libraries will generally have some census records and local newspapers on microfilm. The larger libraries will have a more complete and varied selection. Some libraries have a printed listing of what they have in their microfilm collection. You might want to check to see if the library you are visiting has one. Libraries usually do not loan out microfilm.

Besides their availability at local libraries, you can rent or purchase many types of microfilms from the National Archives or a private company (e.g. AGLL). If your local library doesn't have the census record for Lafourche Parish in 1830, for example, you can order it from one of these places and use the microfilm for as long as one month for two to three dollars per roll. Your library may even be able to order it for you.

CENSUSES

From 1810 to the present, U.S. censuses were taken in Louisiana. These are available on microfilm. Many of the parish and state censuses have been indexed and some have been published in their entirety. Earlier censuses were taken sporadically in Louisiana in the eighteenth century. These have been published in several books. Four early Acadian censuses (1671, 1678, 1686, 1714) have been published. Censuses usually give the name of the head of the household and the number of people in certain age ranges. Some censuses list other members of the household, ages, and so forth. More detailed information on each census can be found in the chapter covering the time period of that census.

Before we start, let me say one thing about documentation. Remember to write EVERYTHING down. Do not neglect information which may be contrary to what you already have . . . it may later turn out to be the correct version. And **please** write down where you get the information. Once you accumulate hundreds of pieces of data (and it doesn't take long), you will not be able to remember where everything came from if you or someone else needs to know. You should also write down when the information was obtained and from what location. There are spaces on the forms in this book in which to put the reference sources. Please use them.

III

1921 TO TODAY

Why select the years "1921 to Today"

The latest U.S. census that has been released (March, 1992) is the 1920 census. For reasons of privacy, census results are not released until 72 years (about the average human life span) has gone by. There is not much published material (e.g. church records) to go by in this time period. There should still be someone around who can remember information on people who existed back to 1920.

This just might be the easiest chapter to get through . . . or it could be the hardest. In other words, if you cannot get out of the starting gate, it'll be hard to finish the race. So, get your pencil and charts ready, and let's see if we cannot get those first few generations of ancestors without hitting any brick walls!

FAMILY & PERSONAL DOCUMENTS

Okay . . . you're ready for your first chart. Put down your names and your parents' names and the vital statistics. Almost everyone should know this basic data. (Special cases such as adoption are not in the scope of this book. Other material is available for such cases. Adoptees can also try the National Adoption Registry at 1-800-875-4347.) Most people also know information on their grandparents (at least their names and approximate age). Any other information . . . great-grandparents, where these ancestors lived, etc. . . . should be written down at this time, even if you are not sure. Some people may be able to completely fill their four generation chart, while others might get stuck at their grandparents. If you're one of the lucky ones who's gotten back to great-grandparents or further, do not go away. You might need to pay attention so you can learn how to corroborate your data.

Next, consult your relatives. Start with your parents and grandparents (if they are still around). Then try collateral relatives . . . aunts, uncles, cousins, etc. First ask around to see if anyone has done any work on your family's ancestry. There's usually someone in the family (even though it may be a third cousin) who's worked on it. Of course, it won't solve all your problems. A second cousin, for example, will only have 25% of their ancestry in common with you. But if your problem lies in that 25%, you've got it made. Sometimes you may even find that information on a branch of your family has been published. If you cannot find a collateral relative whose done genealogical work, do not despair. There's still a wealth of information available from collateral relatives. Find the oldest ones (e.g. a great aunt) and ask them for help. But be careful.

Don't just show up on their doorstep, tape recorder in hand, and throw a hundred difficult questions in their face. That doesn't help either of you. Call or write first and arrange to "have a chat" about your relatives. Don't start out with a barrage of questions. Engage in light conversation to get them at ease. Remember, if you are consulting them about old information, they are probably getting on in years themselves. Treat them with the respect they deserve. It may require several visits to get the information you need.

Recording a conversation is the easiest way to make sure you do not miss anything; but some people may not want to be recorded. If you must record the conversation, ask for permission first. It would be best to use a microcassette recorder that you can put in your pocket so as not to inhibit them.

Begin with simple questions. "What were your parents' names? Where were they from? What do you recall about your sister (my grandmother)?" You can gradually move into the harder questions such as "When and where were your parents born? Who were your grandparents?" and so on. It may help to ask a question a couple of different ways if they cannot come up with anything the first time. Remember to write down everything, even if it contradicts information you may already have.

And do not stop at one relative. Any one collateral relative can just help you with those ancestors that you have in common. Try to contact as many collateral relatives as you can on every branch of your family. That third cousin of yours that you've never met may just have the missing piece to your puzzle.

You may have to start a phone or letter-writing campaign. If your relatives live elsewhere and traveling to see them is not possible, you'll need to phone or write them. If phoning, use techniques similar to the face-to-face interview. If writing, be sure to include a self-addressed stamped envelope to get the quickest and best responses.

Let's say we've hit a wall (or need to confirm our memory). Maybe your grandmother died when your parent was a child. Maybe a great-grandfather moved to town from another city. There are a multitude of roadblocks that can come up (both now, and as we go further back in time). Where do we go for help?

Look around for any documentation that you, your parents, or other relatives may have. This could be a family Bible, old birth certificates, marriage licenses, old letters, etc. If personal interviews and documents do not turn up any clues, you'll need to go outside your family.

COURTHOUSE

What if you're still stuck? Now you're going to have to consult printed material that is harder to obtain or to search through. Let's say you get stuck on your grandmother. You cannot find who her parents were. First go to the courthouse in the parish where she was married. You might have to try several parishes if you are not sure of the exact location. Most parishes have an index to the marriage licenses. Check the index first. Remember to look under her maiden name. What if you cannot find your grandmother listed? Check your grandfather's name. Also check for name variations. They might have mispelled your grandmother's name. Once you find the license location, get the book containing that license (or have a staff member get it). You will want to see if her parents are listed on the marriage license. Sometimes parents are listed and sometimes not.

The courthouse contains other records that might help you. After checking the marriage records, check the conveyance books, successions/wills/probates, and civil suits. They are not ideal genealogical records, but they may be of some help. Successions, wills, and probates relate to a person's death and may mention the children. Remember to first check the indexes if they are available.

CHURCH RECORDS

You may need to check the church records. Non-Catholic church records can usually be found at the church where the event occurred. The condition of these records varies widely from church to church. Catholic church records for the twentieth century are not in print (as are earlier records) and are located in the church that produced them (instead of the diocesan archives, as are earlier records). (Some twentieth century church records are in print in periodicals. Consult the periodical index.)

Go to the church in which the persons in question were married and get a copy of their marriage certificate. Some churches have the marriages listed in book form. You will be looking for the parents on the marriage record. If you couldn't find out which church it was, you may need to try several churches. The diocesan archives may be able to help you track down Catholic records. Information on the different dioceses can be found in Chapter 2.

You can also check the baptismal records. These almost always give the parents and may give other relatives. Again, this may require going to several churches; but first check the churches in which you think they were baptized.

VITAL RECORDS

If you have SOME information on a person, you can try to get a copy of their vital records. These include birth, marriage, and death certificates filed with the state. Louisiana has these back to 1914. They have New Orleans records from even earlier (birth-1790, marriage-1830, death-1803). Records for the years before 1940 can be found in the Louisiana State Archives. You can get a copy of the records after 1940 by going to the records office (in the Louisiana State Office Bldg., 325 Loyola, New Orleans); or, you can send in your request by mail.

You must give them enough information to work on . . . they won't go searching through years of records to find something for you. They will look at the given year and one year before and after. So, it is usually better to take care of it in person, as you can adjust the search information on the spot. Try to include: their full name, their parents' names, location, their sex, and their race. You must state your relationship to the person; they won't send them to just anyone . . . only direct relatives.

You have to send your money in with the request. The present cost is $8 for birth certificates and $5 for marriage or death certificates (1991 prices).

CEMETERIES

Cemeteries can be very helpful in this time period. In most cases, the damage done by weathering is not enough to ruin the inscription. First check to see if a listing of the tombstones has been published. Most cemetery lists are in genealogical periodicals, although a few books exist. The cemeteries in Terrebonne Parish, for example, have all been published. Usually the name, birth date, and death date are given (although one or both of the dates may be omitted). First look for the desired names in the index if one exists. Check the location of the tombstones (or written records). Relatives (especially spouses) were often buried side by side.

Another "gruesome" source is the funeral home. Most funeral homes have records of the deaths they've "handled." You may want to check their records, if possible.

NEWSPAPERS

A time-consuming source you may look at is newspapers. These will usually be found in microfilm form. Marriage notices, birth announcements, and obituaries can be found here. This source may require a lot of time, however, if you do not know exactly when or where an event occurred. You may end up looking through years of newspapers to find one obituary. In a few cases (such as *Houma Newspaper Deaths, 1855-1981*), newspaper obituaries have been indexed in book form. If the ancestor in question lived around New Orleans, check the New Orleans Public Library. They have an alphabetized file of all obituaries from the *Times-Picayune*. And remember that many people not living in New Orleans had obituaries in the *Times-Picayune*, especially if they had children in New Orleans or if they died in a New Orleans hospital.

If you still come up dry, try contacting a genealogical society where your relatives lived. Chances are that someone there may be able to help you. You may also want to place a query in genealogical periodicals covering the area in which they lived.

Of course, there are other sources of information, but they may be long shots and may require a bit of work. These include: family history books (library), old phone books (library), military records (courthouse or archives), family histories (library), employment records, voter registration rolls (courthouse), tax lists (courthouse), and so on. See *The Source* for a comprehensive listing of possible sources.

Hopefully, you have filled in most of your first pedigree chart. If you've got events (births, deaths, marriages) before 1920, we can now move on to the next time period. You may get every branch to this point. But, it is more likely that you have hit a "brick wall" ancestor.

No matter where you look, you cannot get any further back on his/her ancestors. We all have these ancestors at one point or another. Hopefully they won't start popping up too soon in your search. If you do get stuck on one or more branches, skip it and go on with those branches on which you have found information. Perhaps later on in your search, as you become more adept at your genealogical skills and are searching through various material, you will find some bit of information that will allow you to break through those brick walls. Be forewarned that you will ultimately find some ancestor(s) that will be a dead end. The information to solve the problem doesn't exist or is hidden away somewhere. We just have to learn to accept it and hope for a lucky break.

So, now we can take our almost completed chart and move on to the next time period. Don't forget about this chapter . . . you may have to come back to it. In fact, as you pick up bits of information you will be moving back and forth through the chapters.

IV

1810 to 1920

Why select the years 1810-1920?

There are two things that characterize this period: U.S. censuses and printed church records. Censuses were done every ten years. This period includes all of the U.S. censuses. Also, many of the Catholic church records from this period have been published, eliminating the need to travel from church to church to find records.

Congratulations! You've made it to the second time period. You are now ready to go back to the beginning of the nineteenth century . . . before Louisiana was even a state. You will be going back further than any of your relatives can remember. Oral testimony of some very old relatives will probably help you only with the latter part of this period. The bulk of your research from now on will now be archival material.

This period should allow you to complete your first four-generation pedigree chart and about half of the second level of charts. This second level is the continuation of your eight great-grandparents from the first pedigree chart. It will consist of one chart for each great-grandparent . . . eight charts in all if you can carry the lineage back through all eight great-grandparents.

CHURCH RECORDS

Let's start this period with church records. Catholic church records have been transcribed and are in print for much of this period; plus, the original records for each diocese are located in one place (the diocesan archives). So, it is often easier to find nineteenth-century church records than it is to find twentieth-century church records. George Bodin's two volumes of *Selected Acadian and Louisiana Church Records* provide a number of records. But a much more complete set of records is found in the four multivolume sets covering the Acadiana area of Louisiana (the "Cajun" parishes).

Southwestern Louisiana comprises the Catholic dioceses of Lafayette and Lake Charles. They include the civil parishes of Acadia, Allen, Beauregard, Calcasieu, Cameron, Evangeline, Iberia, Jefferson Davis, Lafayette, St. Landry, St. Martin, St. Mary, and Vermilion. Church records for these parishes are printed in Rev. Donald Hebert's series *Southwest Louisiana Records*. This is a series of 36 volumes covering 1756 to 1904. The first volume covers the years 1756 to 1810. Each succeeding volume covers a smaller time period (most volumes cover only one or two years). The Appendix has a complete listing of the volumes and the years covered by each.

The Baton Rouge diocese covers the parishes of Ascension, Assumption, East & West Baton Rouge, East & West Feliciana, Iberville, Livingston, Pointe Coupee, St. Helena, St. James, and Tangipahoa. Some of the Florida parishes were not covered in the earlier years. Church records for the Baton Rouge diocese are being printed by the diocese as the *Diocese of Baton Rouge Catholic Church Records*. The thirteen volumes printed so far cover the years 1707 to 1876. Note that the records from 1707 to 1748 (in Volume 1) are Acadian church records that residents of St. Charles-aux-Mines brought with them to Louisiana. The Appendix has a complete listing of the volumes and the years covered by each.

The Houma-Thibodaux diocese covers the parishes of Lafourche, Terrebonne, and the easternmost part of St. Mary. Church records for this diocese are printed in Rev. Donald Hebert's series *South Louisiana Records*. This series of twelve volumes covers the years 1794 to 1903. There is also a series of books, *South Louisiana Vital Records*, published by the Terrebonne Genealogical Society that covers the years 1902 to 1920. The Appendix has a complete listing of the volumes and the years covered by each.

The New Orleans archdiocese covers the parishes around New Orleans, including St. Charles and St. John the Baptist. The diocese is working on the publication of their records. At the present time, they have completed seven volumes of the *Archdiocese of New Orleans Sacramental Records*, spanning the years 1718 to 1803; so this group of books will not be of much help for the time period 1810-1920. You will have to go to the diocese archives for information if it is not in print. Many of the church records for this area from 1810-1920 can be found in other books and periodicals.

First of all, determine which set(s) of books you will need to consult. If you are looking for a birth in Assumption Parish, you will need to look in the Baton Rouge diocese records. If you are looking for a marriage in St. Landry parish, you will need to look in the *Southwest Louisiana Records*. Keep in mind that if you cannot find a record in one set of books, you might want to look in another set. Just as today, people occasionally moved from place to place. Also, parish boundries have changed over the years.

The average birth record (or, more properly, baptismal record) will give the name of the person born, the date of birth and/or baptism, that person's parents, and where the original record can be found. Some records may give godparents, sponsors, or grandparents. You will notice that when parents' names are given, only the first name for the father is given. Since the father's surname is the same as the child's, it is omitted in the transcriptions. The mother's name shows both given names and her maiden name. Occasionally something will be left out. There is nothing more discouraging than finding a birth record that doesn't list one (or both) of the parents. Be sure to distinguish between the birth and baptismal dates. Baptisms usually occurred soon after birth, but they sometimes were done years afterwards. Usually, if only a baptismal record is given, you can assume that the birth occurred a few days or weeks before. A typical birth/baptismal record will look like this.

BOURG, Marie (Joseph & Anne DUGAS) b. 10 June 1844
(SG: v.2, p.41)

This is the record of the birth of Marie BOURG on June 10, 1844, to Joseph BOURG and Anne DUGAS. This record was recorded at St. Gabriel Church on page 41 of volume 2. The church abbreviations are given at the front of each book.

The average marriage record will give the names of the couple, their parents, the date it took place, and where the original record can be found. The parents' names are neglected in marriage records more than in birth records, but usually can be found. A typical marriage record will look like this.

SAVOIE, Rosalie (William & Aimee FOREST) m. 26 May 1867
Jean BERGERON (NI Ch.: v.1, p.12)

This is the church record of the marriage of Jean BERGERON and Rosalie SAVIOE (daughter of William SAVOIE & Aimee FOREST) on May 26, 1867. It was recorded at the New Iberia church, on page 12 of volume 1. Notice that the parents of Jean BERGERON are not given. Sometimes both sets of parents are given, but sometimes only one (or neither) set is listed. If the spouse's parents are not listed, try looking up the record under the spouse's name. For example, the listing for this marriage under "BERGERON, Jean" may give his parents.

The church really did not keep death records. They kept funeral records. These are the least thorough of the church records. Funerals were often not written up in the church records; and in the early days, someone might be dead and buried for weeks before the traveling priest comes by. A typical death record might look like this.

GAUTREAUX, Beloni d. 4 April 1832 at age 82 (SM: v.3, p.67)

The death of Beloni GAUTREAUX on April 4, 1832, was recorded at the St. Martinville church on page 67 in volume 3. He was 82 years old. If the death is of a child or youth, the parents are usually given. Death records of older people usually do not include the parents' names.

All records that exist for a time period/diocese are contained in the four sets of books. So, if it isn't in one of the books, it probably doesn't exist. For example, if your great-grandmother's birth record is not in *South Louisiana Records* Volume 4, and you know she was born in Terrebonne Parish in the year 1865, . . . then that record probably doesn't exist. Remember that it is possible that your ancestors did not register an event with the church or that the record was lost before it could be transcribed. Also, remember that these sets of church records are for Catholic records only. The number of Cajun Protestants even up to 1920 was still small; but you might need to check on this possibility.

Rev. Donald Hebert also includes some civil records in his two series. Marriage licenses and succession records may be found. The succession record may tell about when a person died and may mention other family members. It also tells where the original may be found. The original goes into much more detail. If you need information on someone and find that he/she has a succession, you should go to the courthouse where it's located and view the actual document. They are several pages long in some cases.

Marriage licenses are also included in Father Hebert's books. If you want a photocopy or would like to see the original, he refers you to the courthouse where it can be found. Note that sometimes a marriage is entered twice in Father Hebert's books. One will be the church record and one will be the marriage license record (look at the abbreviation for the reference). The correct date of the wedding will be the church record, since the license may have been obtained days or even weeks before the actual wedding date.

It can be very exciting to actually see the marriage license of your great-great-grandparents. It is not possible, however, to view the original church records. If you find a church record and would like to have a copy, you will need to go to the diocesan archives that is holding that church's records. For about $5, you can get a certified transciption of the record.

As you go through the volumes of church records, be prepared to do some detective work. In some cases, you can trace a family line from 1920 to 1810 in one sitting. But you often hit snags . . . not brick walls necessarily . . . just snags. For example, one person's parents on a marriage record may not be given, you might find the marriage record but no birth record, the records may be under a different name, etc. Things of that kind are going to happen.

Once you've gotten all you can from the church record books, it is time to go on to the censuses. There will be some incomplete lines, but you can come back to them. The censuses and other forms of information should be able to fill some gaps. And do not forget about the church record books . . . you will be coming back to them to fill in gaps left by the other information.

CENSUSES

The other major source to use in this period is the census. In areas not blessed with good church records, this is the major form of data. It can be harder to use, however. You will probably have to learn to use the microfilm reader, if you haven't already done so.

If the census you are interested in is not indexed (in printed book form), you may be in for quite a bit of research time. Several parishes have indexes for various censuses. Some of these indexes are annotated. This means that the compiler has tried to add details as to the identity of the people in the census. Check the Appendix to see which indexes are available. As we go further back in time, you will find more indexes, since the number of people was smaller. Complete Louisiana census indexes are available for the censuses from 1810 through 1870.

Remember that the censuses (and census indexes) do have errors. Many names were misspelled. Ages and dates given for births could be estimations. The census takers could have just passed up a home; or the people (or some of them) weren't home when he passed by. Annotated censuses may have wrong information, also. Take all of the information down . . . but do not be surprised if some of it is incorrect.

Since the censuses were handwritten, you may not be able to understand the writing. If you get to a letter that you simply cannot decipher, try to find that letter in a word that you recognize. You will get the hang of it after a while, though at first it may seem like you are trying to read a foreign language.

Censuses do give us an abundance of information that is too valuable to ignore. But remember not to take census information as written in stone. Try to find primary records (or even other secondary records) to verify census information, if at all possible. Remember to use the information you have collected from church records to help you with your search. You may even find information in a census that will allow you to go back to the church records to find information you missed.

There is one census for each decade, from 1790 to 1990. Since Louisiana wasn't part of the U.S. in 1790 and 1800, there is no Louisiana census for those years. Censuses have been released on microfilm for the censuses from 1810 to 1920. The 1890 census is missing (except for Ascension parish), due to a fire in Washington, D.C. All censuses do not give the same information. You should obtain census forms to help you collect information. Each census has different information. The census forms have spaces for the correct information. A mail order company based in Utah, Genealogy Unlimited, has a good selection of census forms. They offer a pack of forms that includes all of the basic types, including the census forms. If you do not have a local outlet for genealogical materials (ask someone in the local genealogical society), you might want to order some forms. Check the Appendix for other suppliers.

The 1810, 1820, 1830, and 1840 censuses list the head of the household. They do not give the names of anyone else in the family. They do give the numbers of males and females at the residence according to age grouping (males less than 10, males 10-16, etc.). So you can often make a good guess at the identification of the head of the household by matching the family information you already have with the age groupings. Also, the neighbors can help to identify the people/families when matched with other records.

The 1850 and 1860 censuses are important because they are the first U.S. censuses to list all members of the household. They also give the age, sex, color, occupation, and birthplace of each member. The value of their real estate and personal estate is given. (A few other bits of information are also given.) The numbering is by dwelling and by family, as there were sometimes more than one family at one address.

During this time period, there were several agricultural and slave censuses taken. In the census years, mortality tables were kept on the births and deaths in those years. These may be of some help, also.

The 1870 and 1880 censuses were similiar to the 1850/1860 censuses, with a couple of small changes of genealogical significance. The 1870 census includes whether or not the mother and father were foreign born. The 1880 census lists the place of birth of the mother and father, and it gives the relationship of each family member to head of the household.

The 1890 census, except for Ascension Parish, was destroyed by fire.

The 1900, 1910, and 1920 censuses not only give the age of each person, but they also give the month and year in which they were born. They also give: marital status, the number of years married, how many children were born and how many are still living, immigration information, etc. Again, if you would like to see exactly what each census asks for, check a census form or a published index (if one exists).

There is another related source of information known as the Soundex. These microfilms exist for the years 1880, 1900, 1910, and 1920. The census information for all families with children under ten years old have been put in phonetical order. They are grouped by a phonetic code. This helps to correct for misspellings on the part of the census taker. The code consists of a letter and three numbers. The letter is the first letter of the surname. The first three consonant sounds after the first letter each get a one digit number. Consonant blends get the sound of the first letter. If you run out of consonants (e.g. only 1 or 2 consonants after the first letter), use zeros to complete the three digit number. The numbers for each consonant are listed below. Any consonants not listed are ignored.

1 - b, p, f, v
2 - c, s, k, g, j, q, x, z
3 - d, t
4 - l
5 - m, n
6 - r

Examples of the Soundex code for some Acadian-Cajun names can be found in the table on the following page.

Remember that Soundex information exists ONLY for families with children under ten years old. And do not be surprised if you see different names under the same code. That will happen since the codes are phonetic.

Now that you know what we're dealing with, we are ready to begin. Remember to see if the parish in which you are interested has a census index (and for every census as you work back in time). It can save you hours of searching through microfilm.

Start with the 1920 census. If possible, find out which parish ward they lived in. Each parish is divided into several wards. It cuts down on the search time if you can narrow it down to specific wards. Hopefully you will at least know what parish in which to look. If a thorough search in a likely parish comes up dry, do not be surprised if you have to look in other parishes. People moved back then, too.

When you find an ancestor, write down all available information. You may want to write down a few neighbors, too. This may help you later on. For example, if the census taker misspelled your ancestor's name in the 1910 census, it might be hard to find. But if you know several neighbors from 1920, you might be able to find them easier and thereby find your ancestor (if they hadn't moved between 1910 and 1920).

Since the number of years married is often recorded, you can extrapolate the approximate marriage date. Just subtract the number of years married from the date of the census.

If the farthest you could get back to was someone born between 1910 and 1920 (with no knowledge of the parents' names), you can try to find a child of the proper name and age in the area that the person supposedly came from. If this works, try to find other evidence to correlate the data. It is entirely possible to have two people of about the same age with the same name in the same place. You can be better certain of your data if the name is somewhat unique. For example, though there may be five Joseph HEBERTs in the same place at one time, there was probably only one Anselme Onezippe HEBERT around!

Remember to use your common sense. Ten-year-olds do not get married, women did not have children in their sixties, and so on. Most people got married in their twenties (for the first time), give or take a few

SOUNDEX CODES
for Some
South Louisiana Surnames

SURNAME	SOUNDEX	SURNAME	SOUNDEX
ARCENEAUX	A 625	DUCOTE	D 230
ARDOIN	A 635	DUFRENE	D 165
AUCOIN	A 250	DUGAS	D 220
AUTHEMENT	A 355	DUHON	D 500
AUZENNE	A 250	DUPLANTIS	D 145
BABIN	B 150	DUPLECHIN	D 142
BABINEAUX	B 152	DUPRE	D 160
BELANGER	B 452	ESCHETE	E 230
BENOIT	B 530	FALCON	F 425
BERGERON	B 626	FALGOUT	F 423
BERNARD	B 656	FANGUY	F 520
BERTHELOT	B 634	FONTENOT	F 535
BERTRAND	B 636	FORET	F 630
BILLIOT	B 430	FRIEDRICH	F 636
BLANCHARD	B 452	FRUGE	F 620
BONIN	B 550	FUSELIER	F 246
BONVILLAIN	B 514	GAUTHIER	G 360
BORDELON	B 634	GAUTREAUX	G 362
BOUDREAUX	B 362	GIROIR	G 660
BOURGEOIS	B 622	GREMILLION	G 654
BREAUX	B 620	GUIDRY	G 360
BRIGNAC	B 625	GUILLORY	G 460
BROUSSARD	B 626	GUILLOT	G 430
BRUNET	B 653	HAYDEL	H 340
BURAS	B 620	HEBERT	H 163
CASTILLE	C 234	HERNANDEZ	H 655
CENAC	C 520	HIMEL	H 540
CHAMPAGNE	C 512	JARREAU	J 600
CHAUVIN	C 150	JONES	J 520
CHERAMI	C 650	LACOUR	L 260
CHIASSON	C 250	LAFITTE	L 130
COMEAUX	C 520	LANDRY	L 536
CORMIER	C 656	LAPEYROUSE	L 162
CROCHET	C 623	LAVERGNE	L 162

SURNAME...........SOUNDEX	SURNAME............SOUNDEX
DAIGLE....................... D 240	LEBLANC .... L 145
DOIRON...................... D 650	LEBOEUF...................... L 110
DOMINGUE................. D 552	LECOMPTE.................... L 251
DOUCET .... D 230	LEDET............................ L 330
DUBOIS...................... D 120	LEMOINE...................... L 550
LIRETTE...................... L 630	RABALAIS..................... R 142
LOPEZ.......................... L 120	RACHAL........................ R 240
MALBROUGH............. M 416	RHODES........................ R 320
MARCEL .... M 624	RICHARD...................... R 263
MARTIN .... M 635	ROBICHAUX................. R 122
MATHERNE................ M 365	RODRIGUE .... R 362
MAYEAUX................... M 200	ROMERO....................... R 560
MELANCON................ M 452	ROUSSEL...................... R 240
MIRE............................ M 600	ROY .... R 000
MOUTON..................... M 350	SAUCIER .... S 260
NAQUIN .... N 250	SAVOIE .... S 100
NUNEZ........................ N 520	SCHEXNAYDER............. S 253
ORTEGO......................O 632	SMITH .... S 530
OUBRE........................O 160	SOILEAU .... S 400
PATIN.......................... P 350	THERIOT .... T 630
PELLEGRIN................. P 426	THIBODEAUX............... T 132
PICOU.......................... P 200	TOUPS .... T 120
PITRE.......................... P 360	TRAHAN....................... T 650
POCHE......................... P 200	VERRET .... V 630
PORCHE .... P 620	VIDRINE .... V 365
PREJEAN..................... P 625	VOISIN.......................... V 250
PRICE.......................... P 620	WAGUESPACK............. W 221
PRUHDOMME.............. P 635	WEBRE .... W 160
QUEBEDEAUX.............Q 132	WILLIAMS.................... W 452

years. Most children were born to women between the ages of eighteen and forty.

Once you've gotten all possible information from the 1920 census, do the same thing for the 1910 and 1900 censuses. Since they are almost identical, you will be finding the same type of information. You will also encounter the Soundex at this time. The Soundex is most useful if you do not know where an ancestor lived. Instead of going through several parishes, you only have to cover the names in one code. Remember,

Soundex records only exist if there were children under 10 years old in the household.

If all you have to go by is the 1910 census/Soundex, you can subtract ten years from the ages and try to find the people with those ages in the 1900 census/Soundex. If you cannot find an ancestor in the 1900 census, look out. Since the 1890 census was destroyed, you have a twenty year jump back to the previous census.

The next census we come to is the 1880 census (and Soundex). This is the earliest census for which there is a Soundex. Again, the same basic information is found, but with some variation. Since the month and year are not given (just the age), you have to extrapolate to find the year of birth. Remember, the ages are often approximations.

Keep going back to the 1870 census. You do not have information about the relationship to the head of the household any more. Other than that, it's about the same as before. But now we reach our first statewide census index for Louisiana! It is a thick (2") book with small print, so you might need to use a magnifying glass. It tells you where to find a person in the census. So you will need to consult the census microfilm once you get a person's location. Remember to look for alternate spellings. For example, if you cannot find a BOURG ancestor under "BOURG", try looking under "BOURQUE" or "BURG" or "BARK". Once you find a person, the index directs you to the location of that person on the microfilmed census.

Continue to move back through the 1860 and 1850 censuses. Remember to first consult the index. Indexes are available for the entire state for the rest of the censuses we will encounter. Also, more and more parish censuses are available in book form. Check the Appendix. If you just cannot find someone, try to locate them in a more recent census. Then try to establish their location and their neighbors. Now look for the neighbors in the earlier census (and hope no one moved). Try to get as much information as possible from the 1850 census, because earlier censuses give much less information.

Once you get back to 1840, the head of the household is the only name given. Everyone else is just a number in an age group. This is the same for the 1830, 1820, and 1810 censuses. You can still use the information to help you out. For example, you are looking for the family of a Joseph TRAHAN in the 1830 census. You know that he was in his 20s and had been married for a few years. You would look for a Joseph TRAHAN who had a household with one male in the 16-28 year-old range, a female in the same age range, and one or more children in the 0-10 year-old range. A Joseph TRAHAN record with the male and female in the 45 and up range, for example, would not be the Joseph TRAHAN you are looking for. Be aware that variations could occur. Some families contained many more members than just parents and children. A parent (grandparent) living with a family may show up in an older range. Two adult males in the same age range might mean that a brother of the husband or wife is living with them. So, do not ignore the information given by these early censuses.

CEMETERIES

Cemeteries may be useful for this period, especially the latter part. Remember to first check to see if the cemetery in which you are interested has been listed in a publication. Most of the early tombstones are gone or have weathered away. Some or all of the information you find may be illegible. If you do go out to a cemetery and find an old tombstone of an ancestor, copy everything down . . . as it might be gone the next time you see it. You could also take a picture of it or make a rubbing (place paper over the stone and rub a pencil over the lettering).

GENEALOGICAL BOOKS & PERIODICALS

Published genealogical material should now be of some help. The further back you go, the more likely it is that your ancestors will be in a book or periodical article somewhere.

Some books give the ancestors or descendants of a person (or persons). They list hundreds and thousands of people, vital statistics, and how they are related. You can first try the books that have a title with a name you are working on; but do not let that limit your search. Any one book may have hundreds of different surnames. Check the indexes of these books. Some of them are listed in the Appendix, although it is by no means a complete listing. A missing relative may turn up in the least likely place.

Other books list records such as civil records, marriage licenses, and so on. Again, consult the indexes of books that cover areas in which you are working. Since the number of records gets smaller as you go back in time, you will find greater coverage of the earlier records.

Check the *Acadian-Cajun Genealogical Periodical Article Index* to see what information has been published in periodicals. There are many articles not lengthy enough for a book that will help you.   These include genealogies of people/families as well as records.

COURTHOUSE

Courthouses will continue to be a source of information, as they were in the previous period. More material is published in this period, however, because the records do not deal with people that are still living. Check the Appendix and the *Acadian-Cajun Genealogical Article Index* to see if what you need has been published in a book or periodical. If it hasn't, you will have to actually go to the courthouses. The earliest records will often be in French. Fortunately, many of the French acts have been translated into English. Ask someone at the courthouse where the translations are kept.

Father Hebert's books do include marriage licenses from courthouses. See the Church Records section for more details.

Check the indexes for conveyances, successions, etc., for relevant names. They may hold valuable pieces of information.

MILITARY RECORDS

Military records may help during this period. The pertinent wars during this period were the War of 1812, the Civil War, and World War I. Books have been published that list the Louisiana soldiers who participated in the Civil War and the War of 1812. The Louisiana soldiers in the War of 1812 were written up in Marion Peirson's *Louisiana Soldiers in the War of 1812*. Andrew Booth put together a three volume set (*Records of Louisiana Confederate Soldiers*) for the Civil War. Some Acadian-Cajuns briefly served as Union scouts. You may find some mention of them in the Union records. An index of the compiled service records of Civil War veterans is on microfilm and can be found in several places. The compiled service records themselves are kept by the National Archives. Write to the Archives for an NATF Form 26 application to receive these records. The address is : Reference Services Branch (NNIR), General Services Administration, Washington, D. C. 20408.

Of course, there were other wars during this time. These included the Mexican War and the Spanish-American War. You might want to check the records for these wars, especially if there is some evidence that a relative served in them.

One piece of information that may prove useful is the pension. The pension may mention valuable genealogical data. The state archives has pensions and an index to the pensions (for the War of 1812 and the Civil War). Once you have determined that an ancestor was in one of these wars, you may want to get a copy (for $10) of the pension from the Louisiana Archives. Be aware that not all veterans filed pensions.

V

1786 to 1809

Why select the years 1786-1809?

It is in this time period that the Acadians finish moving
around and settle down. The surges of Acadian
immigrants have withered to a trickle of individuals. The
Acadians are starting to mix with the other nationalities
and are getting settled in their new home.

You are now about to enter the eighteenth century. If you've enjoyed it
up to now, just stick with it . . . it gets much more interesting! Some
parts are easy, and some are difficult. This period doesn't have any
particularly good type of resource. Everything comes in bits and pieces.
Let's look at some of the resources we've used up till now.

CHURCH RECORDS

Some church records exist for this period, although many have been
lost. The records that still exist are in the diocesan archives. (There aren't
really any Protestant church records at this time, so all church records from
here on out will be Catholic records.) You aren't allowed access to the
originals, but you can get certified copies at the archives. Also, all of the
records from the four south Louisiana dioceses from this period have been
printed in the four sets of books mentioned in the previous chapter. (New
Orleans has abstracted records in print up to 1803.) These church record
books are your easiest source of information. Please note that you have
reached a period that has published records for the New Orleans archdiocese.

Don't be surprised if you cannot find a record where it should be. There
could be many reasons for this. Some may have been thrown away. Some
events were never recorded. There were fewer priests and churches back then.
Time has taken its toll on many old records and they have literally
disintegrated. Floods and fire have also destroyed a number of records.
Remember that many records have been lost. Also, this period of settling
in meant that many families were moving around, finding a place in which
to settle down; they may not have had time to record an event in the church.
The record may be in another set of books (for another diocese) because of

this moving. If you hit a brick wall, check the other sets of church records for the same time period.

It could be that the priest couldn't find them. There was only about one church for every 500 square miles. The priest would travel around to the different communities. So don't assume that just because a birth record is at Edgard that the parents lived there. They could have lived ten miles away down Bayou Lafourche.

There are several books on marriages in this period (see the Appendix). A couple of them are:

Marriage Dispensations in the Diocese of Louisiana and the Floridas, 1786-1803 (Shirley Chiasson Bourquard).

Marriage Contracts, Wills, and Testaments of the Spanish Colonial Period, 1770-1804 (Charles Maduell).

CENSUSES

Just because there were no U.S. censuses doesn't mean that there weren't *any* censuses. There were a few scattered censuses, which are in print. *Louisiana Census and Militia Lists 1770-1789* (Robichaux) gives censuses from 1777 (New Orleans), 1784 (second German Coast), 1770 (below New Orleans), and 1789 (Lafourche). It also provides militia lists from 1770 (New Orleans and the German Coast), and 1785 (St. Charles parish). *Colonial Settlers Along Bayou Lafourche, 1770-1798* (Robichaux) gives censuses from 1788 (Lafourche parish), 1791 (Lafourche Des Chetimachas), 1795 (Bayou of Valenzuela), 1797 (Valenzuela in Lafourche parish), and 1798 (Lafourche parish). All residents of the household, their ages, and other ancillary information are given. *Some Late Eighteenth Century Louisianians: Census Records, 1758-1796* (Voorhies) gives census lists and militia lists for New Orleans, the German Coast, St. Charles Parish, and Lafourche. Some of the censuses listed in this book are given as "Acadian" censuses.

There are also numerous censuses made by the Spanish while in control of Louisiana. They can be found in the Papeles Procedentes de Cuba (PPC). This is a valuable source of information on Louisiana during the Spanish control of Louisiana. Unfortunately, these are only available on microfilm and are written in Spanish and French. Some portions have been translated and printed in periodicals.

LAND RECORDS

Since many Acadians had recently moved into the area, there are land records for the property they are claiming. Acadians were moving into three basic areas: Attakapas area, the Acadian Coast, and Bayou Lafourche. Some of them moved westward to the Attakapas District around Opelousas and St. Martinville. Some of them were settled by the Spanish along the Mississippi River. This "Acadian Coast" was upriver from the German Coast. After a while, some of the Acadian Coast residents moved down Bayou Lafourche and settled there. Many of the passengers on the seven ships also settled along Bayou Lafourche in 1785.

When Louisiana was purchased by the United States, they wanted to verify the ownership of land granted by the Spanish government. So, the settlers had to prove that they had been on the land and had cultivated it for ten years. This verification was done in the first decade of the nineteenth century. The *American State Papers* lists these records and are available at several libraries and courthouses in book and microfilm form. An index to them, titled *Grassroots of America* (Phillip McMullin) is also available. But you don't have to search through microfilm if the land you are interested in was in the territory of Orleans (which encompassed most of the Acadian - Cajun parishes). Charles R. Maduell took the *American State Papers* from this area and published them in a book, *Federal Land Grants in the Territory of Orleans: the Delta Parishes*. It covers the Acadiana area of Louisiana, except the Attakapas and Opelousas districts. It separates the land grants by geographical area. Each area has its own cross index, and the land claimants are listed in alphabetical order (by geographical area). So, don't look at the index in the back of the book and expect to find a complete index. If you aren't sure which area an ancestor settled in, you will have to look at all of the indices. The same information can be found in *First Settlers of the Louisiana Territory* (Ericson & Ingmire).

So that you can better visualize what you are researching, here is a brief explanation of land grants. Early in Louisiana's history, everyone settled along the waterways. They would be given long, rectangular sections of land with one of the short sides along the river. The typical size was 6 arpents along the river and 40 arpents deep (1 arpent = 192 feet). To describe the location, you would list the adjacent river, which side of the river you were on, and your neighbors above and below you. By 1807, land not covered by these earlier grants was marked off in squares; this was similiar to the township system used elsewhere.

Some courthouses may have land records from this period. You may want to check there. They will be in the land entries, survey plats, conveyances, and original acts. You might also want to check the State Land Office.

But how can land records help you genealogically? Usually they don't. Occasionally they do give some information (e.g. this land belonging to Jean GIROIR was originally granted to his father, Pierre . . .). It may help, in conjunction with other information, because it can establish the location and neighbors of an ancestor. You can use the land records in conjunction with eighteenth-century censuses and the 1810 census. Also, it can add "color" to your genealogical record; it is interesting to know where your relatives lived 200 years ago.

If your ancestors lived in the Attakapas area (St. Martin, Lafayette, etc.), the *Attakapas Domesday Book* (Conrad) lists land records of the area from 1764-1826. Also, Kenneth Toups has recently translated the first five "cahiers" for Assumption Parish (Assumption Parish, La., Original Cahier Records: Books 1 through 5, 1786-1813). These give land records along Bayou Lafourche from 1786 to 1813.

MILITARY RECORDS

Several militia units were formed in this time period to fight the English. Spain was battling over land with the English at the same time as the American colonists. There are lists of some of these units that can be found in the PPC mentioned earlier. Institutions (such as the DAR) will even accept members whose ancestors belonged to these militias (since they were fighting the English in the Revolutionary War era). Militias were formed both in the Attakapas District and along the Acadian and German Coasts. The lists can be found in the books mentioned previously in the section on censuses. A couple of the books on the Attakapas area are *The Opelousas Post* (DeVille) and *Rapides Post, 1799* (DeVille).

COURTHOUSE/CIVIL RECORDS

Some other civil records do exist. Check with the courthouse of the parish in question to see how far back their records go. One major type of record in this period is the notarial record. In those days, legal transactions were brought to a notary. Of course, most notaries were in New Orleans. The Notarial Archives in New Orleans has scores of documents, but they are in the original handwritten Spanish or French. And, for the most part, they are not indexed. So you are in for a lot of work if you need to search these records. I'd recommend this only if you have been stuck on something for a long time and are willing to spend the time looking for a long shot. Some of the notarial records have been printed. Consult the *Acadian-Cajun Genealogical Periodical Article Index* for articles printed in periodicals. Also, some of the notarial records of one notary have been published in book form. There are 2 volumes of *The Notarial Acts of Estevan de Quinones* (V. 1 - 1778-1784; V. 2 - 1785-1786) compiled by Elizabeth Gianelloni.

Some of the civil records from the German Coast have been published in book form. These include:

St. James Parish Colonial Records, 1782-1787 (Berman)
St. Charles: Abstracts of the Civil Records of St. Charles Parish, 1700-1803 (Conrad)
The German Coast: Abstracts of the Civil Records of St. Charles and St. John the Baptist Parishes, 1804-1812 (Conrad)
St. Jean-Baptiste des Allemands: Abstracts of the Civil Records of St. John the Baptist Parish (Conrad)

GENEALOGICAL BOOKS & PERIODICALS

Genealogical books and periodicals should be of greater help in this period (and even more help in the periods to come). Since the amount of material is smaller and the number of people is fewer, a more complete job has been done for this earlier time period. The major books for this period have been mentioned in the previous paragraphs. Other books contain this period as part of an even larger time span. Consult the Appendix for all of the books that are available and check the *Acadian-Cajun Genealogical Article Index* for periodical articles. Many of the genealogies of people and families cover this period, also.

There is one outstanding book that can be used in this period. It is the *Atlas of Louisiana Surnames of French and Spanish Surnames* by Robert West. It gives the background, including many names and dates, of one hundred families of south Louisiana . . . including Acadian surnames and other nationalities who became Cajuns. It also contains references to the sources and a comprehensive bibliography. Chances are that at least one (and probably more) of your ancestors is in this book. It may be of help in the previous chapter, as it takes some lines into the 1800s. It will also be of help in later chapters, as it often takes the reader back to the first person with that surname. The book is available from the Geoscience Department of Louisiana State University in Baton Rouge.

VI

1755 to 1785

Why select the years 1755-1785?

This is the period of the great deportation. If you haven't read about this part of Acadian history, you are urged to do so now (see the Appendix). The deportations started in 1755 and lasted about eight years. Between 1755 and 1785, the Acadians were nomads . . . looking for a place to settle. The year 1785 marks the last surge of Acadian immigration, when seven ships delivered over 1500 Acadians to Louisiana.

You have now entered the most volatile period of Acadian-Cajun history. Some lines may be easy to trace, while others could easily lead to brick walls. If your ancestors went straight from Acadia to France and then to Louisiana, your job should be simple. If they went to Virginia, and then to England, and then to France, and then to Louisiana . . . then you may have a rough road ahead. But don't get discouraged. You should be able to trace most of them to the next time period.

First, we will introduce you to the different groups of people that we will be dealing with in this period. They are: other nationalities in Louisiana, Acadian settlers in exile (1764-1785), Acadian settlers on the seven ships that arrived in Louisiana in 1785, and Acadian settlers outside Louisiana.

OTHER NATIONALITIES IN LOUISIANA

Before the Acadians began arriving in 1764, some settlers from other countries were third generation Louisianians. French settlers (the military, trappers, farmers, fortune-seekers, etc.) had been settling the area (especially around New Orleans) since the beginning of the century. Check *The First Families of Louisiana* (Conrad) and *First Settlers of the Louisiana Territory* (Ericson and Ingmire) for more information. Since early Louisiana was French, this attracted French-Canadians from Canada during the 1700s. The best information on the French-Canadians can be found in *Le Grand*

Arrangement des Acadiens au Quebec (Adrien Bergeron) and the
genealogical dictionaries by Jette and by Tanguay. The
genealogical dictionaries list ancestors in alphabetical order with
information on their parents, spouses, and sometimes children.
Dates are given when available. The German settlers on the
German Coast (see Ch 7) had been there since the 1720s and were
growing in number. Some Spanish came over when Spain gained
control of Louisiana. But Spain kept Louisiana as it was (mostly
French) and did not try massive settling of their own people. A
particular branch of Spanish people came over from the Canary
Islands from 1778-1783. A few other nationalities (e.g. Africans,
Indians) were also present at this time.

ACADIAN SETTLERS IN EXILE (1764-1785)

The first Acadian settlers arrived in New Orleans in 1764 (see the
Acadian history in the Appendix). Gradually, more and more made
it to Louisiana from other places. The fact that they could settle
on fertile land similiar to their native Acadia and would be near
relatives appealed to many of the exiled Acadians. From 1764 to
1785, over one thousand Acadians settled in two major areas of
Louisiana: the Attakapas District (centered around St. Martinville)
and along the Mississippi River (in an area that became known as
the Acadian Coast).

ACADIAN SETTLERS ON THE SEVEN SHIPS

In 1785, seven ships sponsored by the Spanish government
brought over 1500 Acadian settlers to Louisiana from France. In a
matter of months, the Acadian population in Louisiana had
doubled. The passenger lists for all seven ships have survived and
have been published. These ships marked the last large group of
Acadians to move to Louisiana. Most of the people on these ships
settled in the Lafourche area, though some settled near Baton
Rouge.

ACADIAN SETTLERS OUTSIDE LOUISIANA

Not all Acadians went to Louisiana. Some stayed in the places to which they were exiled. These places include the American colonies, England, France, and the West Indies. Some who had escaped to Canada remained there. Some who were in these lands made their way back to Acadia, now called Nova Scotia. The largest groups of Acadians outside of Louisiana eventually settled in Canada (including Nova Scotia). There was also a significant group who remained in France. For the most part, they were absorbed into their new homeland and its people. (It is in Louisiana where the Acadian culture was dominant.)

For information about these settlers after 1785, you should consult a reference work on the area in which they settled. Information on Acadians who settled in other areas are found mixed in with the general genealogical information of those areas. The *Le Grand Arrangement des Acadiens au Quebec* by Adrien Bergeron gives the direct genealogy for quite a few Canadian-Acadians all the way back to the seventeenth century. The previously mentioned dictionaries by Jette and Tanguay are also helpful for Acadians who settled in Canada. As mentioned in Chapter 1, there are publications on genealogical research in Canada and in Nova Scotia that should be consulted if your Acadian ancestors settled there. If they first went to the American colonies or were in France for a time before returning to Canada, you may find material in the sources listed later in this chapter.

The records for these groups fall into several categories: records in France, records in Louisiana, and records everywhere else. The French records cover the years 1758 to 1785. The Louisiana records cover the years 1764 to 1785 for Acadian settlers and 1755-1785 for settlers of other nationalities. The records from everywhere else cover varying periods of time throughout this period. You will probably have to rely on what has been published, because going to all of the actual record locations would be a tremendous task. Since almost all of the existing material has been published, you won't even be missing out on much. Most of it is in books, although some material may be found in periodicals.

FRENCH RECORDS

Acadians returned to France (their original homeland) a number of ways. Some who were deported in 1755 went to the American colonies, then to England, and then to France. Others who were deported in 1758 went straight to France. The French records are primarily church records. If you haven't done so, you may want to read up on the movement of the Acadians throughout France during this period.

There are several sets of books that contain the French records for the Acadians of this period. Albert J. Robichaux has published three works on this material. Each lists the families in alphabetical order (by head of household) and gives vital statistics on the family members as well as their travels to and from France. *Acadian Exiles in Chatellerault* gives information about the Acadians at Chatellerault from 1773 to 1785. *The Acadian Exiles in Nantes* includes information on the Nantes area for the years 1775 to 1785. *The Acadian Exiles in St. Malo* is a three volume set spanning the years 1758 to 1785. It gives information in two volumes similiar to that of the Nantes and Chatellerault books, but the third volume consists of transcriptions of Acadian marriage records in France. Robichaux also has a book, *Acadian Marriages in France*, that lists the records of the Dept. of Ille-et-Vilaine from 1759 to 1776.

Milton and Norma Reider have published a three volume series entitled *The Acadians in France*. Volume 1 covers the years 1762 to 1776. Volume 2 covers the Belle-Isle-en-Mer Registers. Volume 3 covers the archives of the port of St. Servan.

In 1785, seven ships left France for Louisiana. These ships, sponsored by the Spanish government, brought over 1500 Acadians to Louisiana. The lists of passengers for all seven ships still exist and have been published. *The Crew and Passenger Registration Lists of the Seven Acadian Expeditions of 1785* by Milton and Norma Reider contains the passengers' names, their ages, relationship to the head of the household, and other miscellaneous bits of information. Much of this information is also given in Janet Jehn's *Acadian Descendants, V. 1*. This is an extremely valuable source if your ancestors came over on one of these ships.

LOUISIANA RECORDS

The Louisiana records include church records, civil records, local commandants' reports, provincial administrative correspondence, and some censuses and militia lists. A few calendars have been published that relate local records. You may first want to check the church record books by the diocese and Donald Hebert. There are fewer records for this time period, so it shouldn't take long. Remember to check the different dioceses because the Acadians were just coming in and may have moved around a bit. And, since there were fewer priests and churches, remember that many records may have never been recorded.

Civil records have been published for several of the older parishes. These include the records of St. Charles (Conrad), St. John the Baptist (Conrad), and St. James (Behrman) Parish (see the previous chapter). Remember that many of today's parishes did not even exist at that time. Consult Louisiana maps for the years in which you are interested to determine parish line movements. Books on marriage contracts at the Opelousas Post (Vidrine) and at Attakapas Post (DeVille) have also been published. These books were introduced in the last chapter.

Some censuses and militia lists of the period have been published in:

Louisiana Troops, 1720-1770 (DeVille)
Louisiana Recruits, 1752-1758 (DeVille)
Louisiana Census and Militia Lists, 1770-1789 (Robichaux)
Colonial Settlers Along Bayou Lafourche, 1770-1798 (Robichaux)
Some Late 18th Century Louisianians: Census Records, 1758-1796 (Voorhies)

The latter three books were described in the last chapter. Remember to first look in the indexes (and look under alternate spellings for the names).

There are a variety of other books on the period. The *Attakapas Domesday Book, 1764-1826* (Conrad) covers land grants in that area of Louisiana. There are three books (by Villeré, Din, and Maduell) that cover the Canary Islanders' migration to Louisiana. They even give the passenger lists of the ships bringing the Canary Islanders. The *Atlas of Louisiana Surnames* mentioned in the last chapter contains a wealth of information on one hundred different surnames. *The First Families of Louisiana* (Conrad) and *First Settlers of the Louisiana Territory* (Ericson and Ingmire) contain many names of this period and earlier. (Most of the information in these books is in the form of lists, especially military lists.) Check the Appendix for a more thorough listing of available books.

RECORDS OF AREAS OTHER THAN FRANCE & LOUISIANA

The English created enormous problems for genealogists when they deported the Acadians. Not only did they scatter them all around the Atlantic, but they also broke up many families. You may find quite a few second marriages at this time because spouses were killed by the English, died on their way to a new land, or were separated from their mates forever. As previously mentioned, you would have to devote much travel and time in order to find this material yourself. Fortunately, several books have been written that cover the miscellaneous travels of the Acadians during the period of exile, the most inclusive being those by Hebert and Jehn.

Acadian Exiles in the Colonies by Janet Jehn deals with those Acadians that were deported to the American colonies. It not only gives the Acadian lists/censuses of the colonies; it tries to match Acadians to the lists. This is helpful since most lists did not give the names of the wife and children. They gave the head of the household, if a wife was present, and the number of children. Jehn's book, *Acadian Descendants,* volume 1, also has some information about the exiled Acadians in Maryland.

Acadian Exiles in the American Colonies by Milton and Norma Reider gives lists of Acadians in several of the American colonies that received the deported Acadians. It is similiar to Ms. Jehn's book, but it doesn't try to find the correct identity of the Acadians.

Acadians in Exile by Rev. Donald Hebert covers a wide range of information about the deported Acadians. It is probably the best all-around source for this period. It contains records from Acadia, Canada, Cayenne (South America), France, and the West Indies (Guadeloupe, Martinique, St. Dominigue, and Ste. Lucie). It also has maps, historical material and the Acadian censuses of 1671, 1686, and 1714. At the end of the book is an inventory of documentary sources on the Acadians.

Some of the genealogy in Adrien Bergeron's eight volume set (*Le Grand Arrangement des Acadiens au Québec*) includes this time period. Even if your ancestors did not settle in Canada, you will probably join up with some of the people in this work.

Exile Without an End by Chapman Milling gives an account of the Acadian exiles in South Carolina. Rene Babineau covers Pennsylvanian Acadian exiles in his book *Acadian Exiles in Pennsylvania.*

A microfilm of the French Neutrals (Acadians) in Massachusetts in the years 1755 to 1769 is in the Massachusetts archives (v. 23-24) and in several Louisiana libraries.

Pierre Belliveau has written a book entitled *French Neutrals in Massachusetts*, which is on the Acadians who entered that state during the exile. It is more a narrative on the events that occurred. It does not contain any name lists.

Cyprien Tanguay's *Dictionnaire Généalogique des Familles Canadiennes* and Rene Jette's *Dictionnaire Généalogique des Familles du Québec* mentioned in chapter six deal with the French Canadians. These dictionaries list people and their vital information in alphabetical order. Reginald Olivier has also published a book on the Canadian families that should be helpful (*Your Ancient Canadian Family Ties*). French-Canadians who came to Louisiana can often be found in one or more of these books. Also, some Acadians may turn up in them.

The largest work on the Acadians, Bona Arsenault's *Histoire et Généalogie des Acadiens*, goes through this period. A listing of the contents of each of the six volumes is given in the Appendix. Although it is in French, it won't take you long to figure out a few key words so that you can make out the essence of the information. The same goes for the other French Canadian books. In fact, a booklet has been published (*Index and Key Words to Histoire et Généalogie des Acadiens* by Donald Hebert) that gives you the basics. Arsenault's books will be discussed more thoroughly in the next chapter.

There are a number of other works on the exiled Acadians. These are most likely to be found in the areas (e.g. colonies) in which they were located. Miscellaneous information can be found in material on the general environment. For example, Gipson's history of the British before the American Revolution has some information.

VII

Why select the years "1636 to 1754"

This could be termed the true Acadian period. The first permanent settlers of note began landing in Acadia in the 1630s. These French settlers inhabited the land called Acadia until 1755-1763, at which time they were expelled by the British. It is very difficult to get further back than these first settlers, though it can be done for a few cases.

The resources for this period are not numerous. But, on the other hand, you are dealing with a smaller group of people. For example, the population of Acadians during this period was never more than 20,000. The bulk of information from this period comes from the church records and censuses. This period covers the original Acadians when they inhabited Acadia and the Cajun ancestors of others in Louisiana in the 1700s. Information on the Louisiana ancestors will be dealt with first.

LOUISIANA "CAJUN" ANCESTRY

There are two major groups of Cajun ancestors in Louisiana in this time period. These are the Germans and the French (and French-Canadians). The Germans arrived in the Mississippi Valley circa 1721 bound for the John Law concession in Arkansas. Instead of going up the Arkansas River, they were forced to settle along the Mississippi River above New Orleans. A census taken in 1724 lists these first settlers. This census, and other information about these German Coast settlers, can be found in J. Hanno Deiler's *Settlement of the German Coast of Louisiana*. Dr. Helmut Blume's *The German Coast During the Colonial Era, 1722-1803* also includes useful information on the settlement of the German Coast. Some of their church records can be found in the published church records. Some civil records are also published. The book on St. Charles parish (Conrad) has civil records back to 1700. Check the Appendix and the periodical index for more sources.

The French were coming to Louisiana since France controlled the area for much of this period. Some were part of the military force, while others came to the New World for business. *The First Families of Louisiana* (Conrad) and *First Settlers of the Louisiana Territory* (Ericson and Ingmire) mentioned in the last chapter are useful here. The French-Canadians were making their way down to Louisiana to join their French counterparts. They also start showing up in this period in the church and civil records. The genealogical dictionaries (by Tanguay and Jette), Reginald Olivier's book, and Adrien Bergeron's eight volume set are your best bets for French-Canadian ancestors of this period. The *Atlas of Louisiana Surnames* includes some of the French-Canadian, French, and Spanish surnames. All four of these books have been previously introduced, but they cover more than one time period. See Chapter VI for other books that go back to this time period.

ACADIAN ANCESTRY

The starting date of this time period, 1636, was chosen because that is when the ship *St. Jehan* arrived with French settlers. An issue of *Acadian Genealogy Exchange* (V. 6, #4) contains an article on the *St. Jehan*. Most of the people from this ship had no families or left no descendants in the area. Only three of them can be found in Acadia later on (Isaac PESSELEY, Pierre MARTIN, and Guillaume TRAHAN). The first groups of permanent settlers began arriving a few years later. Earlier information may be available because church records may mention the settlers' parents' names.

Church Records

There are several books which contain the Acadian church records from this period. The first volume of the Baton Rouge Diocese records contains the records of St. Charles-aux-Mines (1707-1748) that the residents brought with them to Louisiana. More often than not, however, Acadian church records were lost or burnt by the British.

Several books are available that list the other surviving church records. Winston DeVille's *Acadian Church Records, V. 1* lists records from 1679-1757. The Reiders have published four more volumes of Acadian church records. These volumes contain records for: Beaubassin, 1712-1748 (V. 2), Port Royal, 1702-1721 (V. 3), Port Royal, 1716-1729 (V. 4), and Port Royal, 1730-1740 (V. 5). All of the Acadian church records not covered by these works have been destroyed or lost.

Censuses

There were a number of censuses during this period. The most important of these are the censuses of 1671, 1678, 1686, and 1714 . . . all of which have been published in books or periodicals. There were other censuses (which are on microfilm), but they are often of limited help and not readily accessible.

The 1671, 1686, and 1714 censuses are in *Acadians in Exile* (Hebert). The 1671 census can be found in *Les Origines Francaises des Premieres Familles Acadiennes* (Bujold & Caillebeau). The 1671 census is also in periodicals . . . *Acadian Genealogy Exchange* V. 5, #4; *Acadiana Profile* V. 10, #6. The 1678 census can be found in *Acadian Genealogy Exchange* V. 8, #2; *French-Canadian and Acadian Review* V. 7, #1, and *Memoires de la Societe Genealogique Canadienne-Francaise* V. 22, #4. The 1686 and 1714 censuses can be found in *Acadian Genealogy Exchange* V. 8, #4.

The 1714 census contains the names of the heads of the household, the number of males, and the number of females in household. There are names for other family members only for the Beaubassin area of the 1714 census. Like the early U.S. censuses, the 1714 census is of limited use. The three earlier censuses, however, contain names and ages for everyone in the household. Working back in conjunction with the church records and Arsenault's books, these three censuses should help you to trace what you have back to 1671.

Once we get to a parent in the 1671 census, we usually have ended our search for that family line. Very sketchy information exists before this time. It is still not known exactly where the original settlers came from, although many say that Charles de Menou recruited many of them from villages around his land south of Loudun, France, during the 1630s and 1640s. Material by Geneviève Massignon and Nicole Bujold & Maurice Caillebeau has tried to prove this, but no firm evidence exists.

Genealogical Books and Periodicals

There are a few other books and a number of periodical articles on these early years. Consult the *Acadian-Cajun Genealogical Periodical Article Index* for the articles that are available. Don't forget about the *Atlas of Louisiana Surnames*. Its information also includes this period. Some early Acadian notarial records can be found in *Loppinot Papers, 1687-1710* (De Ville).

The books in this period are large works that utilize records that the average person never gets to see. The authors have done much of the difficult work for you.

The two major sets of books by Bergeron and Arsenault have been introduced previously. Adrien Bergeron's *Le Grand Arrangement des Acadiens au Quebec* is an eight-volume set that traces the ancestry of Acadians (who settled in Quebec) all the way back to the first settlers. Even though your ancestors may have gone elsewhere, you will eventually merge into the genealogies in these books. Although written in French, it is easy to follow the genealogies.

The other major work is Bona Arsenault's *Histoire et Généalogie des Acadiens*. The first volume is a history of the Acadian people. It is also available separately in an English translation. Volumes two through six give the genealogy of the Acadians from the original settlers through the end of the eighteenth century. They are in French, but you can get most of the data with just a few translated words. Donald Hebert has an index and list of key words (translated into English) that will help you. Most records give the names and birthdates of a family. Sometimes information concerning family movements are given. A separate index of names has been published by Phoebe Chauvin Morrison (*Index to Bona Arsenault's Histoire et Généalogie des Acadiens*). Of course, such a large work is not without its faults. There are quite a few errors. The periodical, *Acadian Genealogy Exchange*, has been collecting the errors. Janet Jehn has published them in one volume, *Corrections to Arsenault's Histoire et Généalogie des Acadiens*.

There are other books that may be of help, though they do not list person after person as the previous books do. One example is Thomas Akins' book, *Acadia and Nova Scotia: Documents Relating to the Acadian French and the First British Colonization of the Province, 1714-1758*.

The Centre d'Etudes Acadiennes is working on a comprehensive work (*Dictionnaire Genealogique des Familles Acadiennes*) that will cover all of the Acadians. It will be published in phases, with the first phase due out in the early 1990s. The first publication will include Acadian information for about the first seventy-five years of the Acadian settlement. This massive work should answer most of your questions about the early Acadian settlers (if they can be answered).

VIII

PUTTING IT ALL TOGETHER

By now, you should have some ancestors all the way back to the 1600s. Congratulations! But you also have many gaps in your genealogical lineage. Some may be filled after a few more hours of research, while others may never be solved. Since you now have a framework of knowledge to work from, you should now set about finding those missing ancestors. It might be a good idea to make a list of what you are missing.

Going back, generation by generation, list the vacancies in names and other pieces of information. Copy down the information associated with the vacancy and circle or underline the part you are missing. Also put the chart number where the people are located and their Ahnentafel number. You can include more information as needed. An example is given below.

5th GENERATION

Chart # 2

    #16 John BRUN (s/o Simon & Marie BOURG) b. 14 NOV 1876
    #17 Mary SIRE (d/o _____ & _____) b. 3 SEP 1880

6th GENERATION

Chart #4

    #44 Jean BABIN (s/o Michel & _____) b. _____
    #45 Claire _____ (d/o _____ & _____) b. _____

Now you don't have to look through pages and pages of charts for the empty spots to fill. You have a shorter list of key names to concentrate on. You may even start looking through the indexes of miscellaneous books and periodicals for these names. Try placing queries in genealogical periodicals. Unless that particular person has everyone stuck, you should find some help.

You may also want to rewrite your charts. There will be erasures and marks strewn about your working charts. If you plan to show off your charts, you may want to make a neat copy. Also, you can put the information on a wall chart for display. These charts may include four to eight or more generations.

Once you accumulate a few hundred ancestors, you may decide to publish your work . . . either for your family or commercially. You should at least make a few copies to hand out to your family. The most cost efficient way to do this is to have photocopies made at a copy shop. You can also have them bound or you can just put them in a three-ring binder. Ask the copy shop nearest you for a quote on printing prices and the binding methods they offer. Everton Publishers offers a similar service (see any issue of *The Genealogical Helper*). For seven cents per impression (fourteen cents back and front), they will copy your manuscript and even bind it for you. (1993 prices)

If you decide to publish your work commercially, you will probably have to pay the costs yourself. Publishers rarely accept family histories. There are a number of companies that will print and bind your book for you. Some of them are listed in the Appendix. The prices vary widely, depending on the book size, type of cover, type of paper, type of binding, and number of books you require. The larger the page size . . . the more expensive the cost. Hard covers cost at least five dollars more per book than softcovers. Heavier paper (60-70#) costs more than regular paper (50#). Acid-free paper, which lasts for hundreds of years, costs more than regular paper. Stitch binding costs more than stapling or glueing. The more books you have printed . . . the less each book costs.

Be sure you take all costs into account when figuring the cost per book. These costs may involve: typing, setting up photographs, collating, binding, and shipping. Dogwood Printing, for example, will produce 200 softcover copies of an 8 1/2 by 11 inch, 100 page book for $3.22 per book (1993 price). They are one of the less costly publishers. If you have a more sophisticated book in mind, you might want to check out someone like Gateway Press or Anundsen Publishing. Anundsen will publish 200 copies of an 8 1/2 by 11 inch, 150 page book on 60# acid-free paper for $7.67 per book ($4.62 each for 6 by 9 inch size). This price includes set-up charges for 40 photographs and a softcover binding. They will publish 100 copies of the same book in hardcover for $13.81 per book ($10.66 each for 6 by 9 inch size [1993 prices]). As you can see, hard covers and a smaller printing volume will definitely raise the price per book.

Send the prospective publishers the information on your book (number of pages, size of the book, type of cover, number of books to be printed) and they will send you a current price quote. Try to order more books than you think you will need, since the price per book goes down as the quantity increases. If you underprint, it will cost you much more to print just a few more copies later on.

Several books have been written on publishing. *Publishing Short-Run Books* by Dan Poynter gives you details on the printing and binding methods available. *How to Publish and Market Your Family History* by Carl Boyer gives you information on how to put together a genealogy book and sell it. Some of the publishers (such as Anundsen Publishing and Genealogy Publishing Service) put out literature that can help the prospective author. Check the Appendix for a listing of publishers.

APPENDIXES

A: Helpful Hints

B: Genealogy Forms

C: Maps

D: Reference Sources

E: The History of Acadians and Cajuns

F: Acadian-Cajun Timeline

G: Canadian and Louisiana Genealogical Societies and Their Publications

H: Libraries with Significant Acadian-Cajun Resources

I: Genealogical Supply Companies

J: Louisiana Genealogical Travel Guide

K: Acadian Genealogical Travel Guide

73

APPENDIX A

HELPFUL HINTS

-> Be aware of name variations.

>> Given and surnames may have different spellings. Sometimes people were called by their middle name.

-> Use common sense.

>> People usually married for the first time when they were 18 to 30 years old. Women had children from shortly after their marriage until they were about forty years old.

-> Look at neighbors.

>> People often married their neighbors. Knowing neighbors can also help you find someone if they have been left out or misidentified in a census.

-> Use collateral relatives.

>> Records of ancestors' siblings, cousins, etc., may include vital information on other ancestors in your lines.

-> Use indexes.

>> Check to see if an index is available before you start searching a census. Also, you may want to look through the indexes of genealogical books for those surnames in which you are interested.

-> Look at changes in territorial lines.

>> Be aware of parish boundary movements. You could spend hours of wasted time searching parish records for an event that occured in another parish.

-> Use abbreviations.

>> You will be gathering a lot of information . . . raw data and references. Using abbreviations will save you time and will be easier on your hand.

-> Be aware of the family characteristics.

> People had large families. Sometimes siblings had the same first name and different middle names. If a child/infant died, a child born later may be given the same name. Women might still have kids into their 40's. It was not uncommon for someone to be married more than once. Divorce was not as common, but the death of a spouse in olden times was more prevalent. It was not unusual for a remarriage to occur quickly . . . to obtain a mother for the children or to obtain a father to take care of the family.

APPENDIX B

GENEALOGY FORMS

1) Four Generation Pedigree Chart

2) Family Group Chart

These forms can be enlarged as necessary to fit a full page. If you would like originals, please send a self-addressed, self-stamped envelope to the author and he will send you a free copy of each. If you would like more than one copy, they are available from the author for $5.00 per 100. (T. Hebert, P.O. Box 1416, Houma, LA 70361.)

GENEALOGY FORM

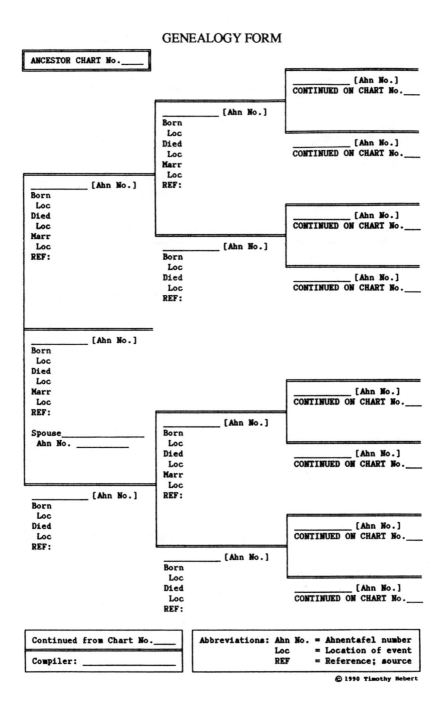

ANCESTOR CHART No.____

_____ [Ahn No.]
Born
 Loc
Died
 Loc
Marr
 Loc
REF:

_____ [Ahn No.]
Born
 Loc
Died
 Loc
Marr
 Loc
REF:

_____ [Ahn No.]
Born
 Loc
Died
 Loc
Marr
 Loc
REF:

Spouse_____
 Ahn No. _____

_____ [Ahn No.]
Born
 Loc
Died
 Loc
REF:

_____ [Ahn No.]
Born
 Loc
Died
 Loc
Marr
 Loc
REF:

_____ [Ahn No.]
Born
 Loc
Died
 Loc
REF:

_____ [Ahn No.]
CONTINUED ON CHART No.___

_____ [Ahn No.]
CONTINUED ON CHART No.___

_____ [Ahn No.]
CONTINUED ON CHART No.___

_____ [Ahn No.]
CONTINUED ON CHART No.___

_____ [Ahn No.]
CONTINUED ON CHART No.___

_____ [Ahn No.]
CONTINUED ON CHART No.___

_____ [Ahn No.]
CONTINUED ON CHART No.___

_____ [Ahn No.]
CONTINUED ON CHART No.___

Continued from Chart No.____

Compiler: _____

Abbreviations:	Ahn No.	= Ahnentafel number
	Loc	= Location of event
	REF	= Reference; source

© 1990 Timothy Hebert

GENEALOGY FORM

FAMILY GROUP CHART

HUSBAND _____ See Chart No.____
Ahnentafel No._____ Occupation _____
Born _____ Place _____ Source _____
Marr _____ Place _____ Source _____
Died _____ Place _____ Source _____
Father _____ Ahnentafel No._____ See Chart No.____
Mother _____ Ahnentafel No._____ See Chart No.____
Husband's Other Wives _____

WIFE _____ See Chart No.____
Ahnentafel No._____ Occupation _____
Born _____ Place _____ Source _____
Died _____ Place _____ Source _____
Father _____ Ahnentafel No._____ See Chart No.____
Mother _____ Ahnentafel No._____ See Chart No.____
Wife's Other Husbands _____

CHILDREN'S NAMES see Chart No.→	BIRTH DATE/PLACE	MARRIED TO: NAME/DATE/PLACE	DEATH DATE/PLACE

→ Check off this box if this child has his/her own Family Group Chart.

MISC NOTES:

APPENDIX C

MAPS

1) Acadia, circa 1720

2) The Atlantic, circa 1755-1785

3) France, circa 1775

4) Louisiana, 1765-1785

ACADIA, ca. 1720

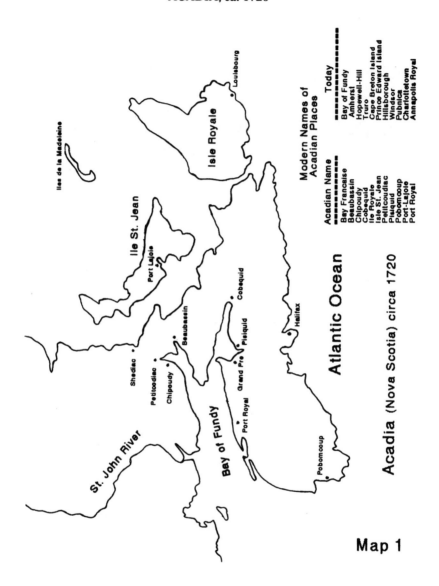

Map 1

The Atlantic, 1755-1785

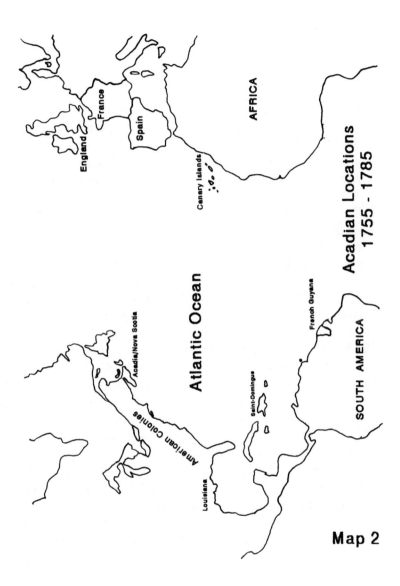

Map 2

France, ca. 1775

France (circa 1775)   **Map 3**

Louisiana, 1765-1785

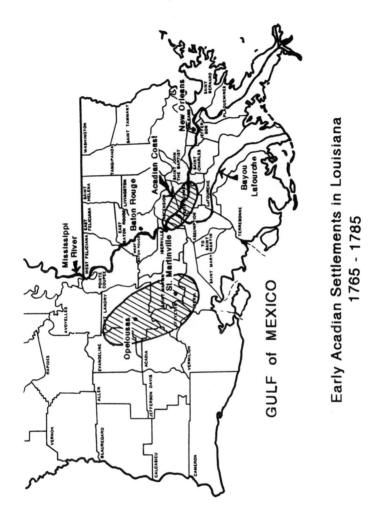

Map 4

APPENDIX D

REFERENCE SOURCES

Note that many books do not have a publisher (e.g.. Milton and Norma Reider's material). Genealogy books are often published by the author. If the publisher is not given, then it was probably published by the author(s). Some books, where an author's name is not given, were compiled by a genealogical society.

They are divided into four sections. The first section is the general section that has the most genealogical information. The second section is on background material. The third section is reference material. The fourth section consists of books on certain family names.

Acadia Parish, LA Cemetery Listings, V. 1
     Pointe de l'Eglise Historical & Genealogical Society
     (Church Point, LA: L'Acadie Publishing Company, 1991)

Acadian Church Records, V. 1: 1679-1757
     Winston De Ville (Cottonport, LA: Polyanthos, 1975)

Acadian Church Records
 V. 2: Beaubassin, 1712-1748
 V. 3: Port Royal, 1702-1721
 V. 4: Port Royal, 1716-1729
 V. 5: Port Royal, 1730-1740
     Milton and Norma Reider (1976 ->)

Acadian Descendants
 *V. 1: Acadian Genealogy & History, Maps, Acadian Exiles, Seven
  Ships Passenger Lists, Photocopies of Early Documents* (1972)
 V. 2: Descendants of Jean Gaudet and His Two Wives (1975)
 V. 3: Descendants of Daniel LeBlanc/Marie Bourgeois (1979)
 V.4: Pedigree Charts from the Acadian Genealogy Exchange (1980)
 V. 5: Descendants of the Families of Michel and Pierre Forest (1984)
 V.6: Pedigree Charts from the Acadian Genealogy Exchange (1982)
 V. 7: Descendants of Rene Forest/Francoise Dugas (1987)
 V. 8: Descendants of Gabrielle Forest/Pierre Brasseaux (1991)
     Janet Jehn (Acadian Genealogy Exchange: Kentucky)

Acadian Exiles in the Colonies
Janet Jehn (Kentucky: Acadian Genealogy Exchange)

Acadians in Exile
Donald Hebert (Hebert Publications, 1980)

Acadian Exiles in the American Colonies
Milton Reider (1977)

Acadian Exiles in the Golden Coast of Louisiana
Sidney Marchand (Donaldsonville, LA, 1943)

The Acadian Exiles in Nantes, 1775-1785
Albert Robichaux (1978)

The Acadian Exiles in Chatellerault, 1773-1785
Albert Robichaux (Hebert Publications, 1983)

The Acadian Exiles in St. Malo, 1758-1785
Albert Robichaux (Hebert Publications, 1981)

Acadian marriages in France, 1759-1776
Albert Robichaux (N.O. Bicentennial Commission, 1976)

Acadian Pedigree
J. Cleveland Fruge

The Acadians in France: V. 1, 1762-1776
Milton Reider (1967)

The Acadians in France: V. 2, Belle Isle en Mer Registers
Milton Reider (1972)

The Acadians in France: V. 3, Archives of the Port of St. Servan
Milton Reider (1973)

The Acadians of Prince Edward Island
Joseph Henri Blanchard (LeDroit and Leclerc: Ottawa, Ontario, 1964)

Ancestor Charts and Tables (2 volumes: 1985 & 1988)
(Lake Charles, LA: Southwest Louisiana Genealogical Society)

Assumption Parish, Louisiana Original Cahier Records: Books 1 thru 5,
1786-1813
Kenneth Toups (Thibodaux, LA: Audrey Westerman Publ., 1991)

Atlas of Louisiana Surnames of French and Spanish Origins
Robert West (Baton Rouge, LA: Geoscience Publ., LSU, 1986)

The Attakapas Domesday Book: V. 1, 1764-1826
Glenn Conrad (Lafayette, LA: Center for Louisiana Studies, 1990)

Attakapas Post: The Census of 1771
Winston De Ville (1986)

An Attempt to Reassemble the Old Settlers in Family Groups
Sidney Marchand (Baton Rouge, LA: Claitor's, 1965)

Baie Des Chaleurs Registres, 1786-1799
Janet Jehn (Kentucky: Acadian Genealogy Exchange, 1984)

Baie Ste. Marie Parish Registres, 1799-1801
Janet Jehn (Kentucky: Acadian Genealogy Exchange)

Be It Known and Remembered (4 volumes)
LA Genealogical and Historical Society (1960, 1961, 1962, 1967)

Book of Charts (3 volumes)
Terrebonne Genealogical Society (Houma, LA: 1987, 1989, 1990)

Brand Book for Opelousas and Attakapas District, 1739-1744

Burial Records of St. Andrew, St. Lawrence, and St. Patrick
Terrebonne Genealogical Society (Houma, LA: 1989)

Calender of Louisiana Colonial Documents
V. 1 - Avoyelles Parish

V. 2 - St. Landry Parish
V. 3 - St. Charles Parish
    Winston De Ville (Baton Rouge, LA: State Archives and Records
        Commission, 1964)

Canary Islands Migration to Louisiana, 1778-1783
    Sidney Villere (New Orleans, LA: Genealogical Research
        Society of N.O., 1971)

Canary Islands Migration to Louisiana, 1778-1783
    Charles Maduell

Cemeteries of Central Lafourche Parish
    Traise Hebert (Thibodaux, LA: Audrey Westerman Publ., 1984)

Cemeteries of East Ascension Parish, LA
    Doris Millet Melancon and Elsie Moore Little (1990)

Cemeteries of Houma, LA
    Terrebonne Genealogical Society (Houma, LA: 1989)

Cemeteries of Lower Lafourche Parish, LA
    Terrebonne Genealogical Society (Houma, LA: 1990)

Cemeteries of Lower Terrebonne Parish
    Terrebonne Genealogical Society (Houma, LA: 1990)

Cemeteries of Upper Terrebonne Parish
    Terrebonne Genealogical Society (Houma, LA: 1990)

Civil War Records at the Louisiana State Archives
    Arthur Bergeron (Baton Rouge, LA: Lecomite des archives de
        la Louisiane, 1981)

The Civil War Tax in Louisiana, 1865
    John Milton Price (Cottonport, LA: Polyanthos, 1975)

Colonial Land Grants in the Attakapas
    Gertrude Taylor

Colonial Louisiana Marriage Contracts (4 volumes)
Winston De Ville (Baton Rouge, LA: Claitor's, 1962)

Colonial Settlers Along Bayou Lafourche, 1770-1798
Albert Robichaux (1974)

Computer Indexed Marriage Records for various parishes
Nicholas Murray (Hunting for Bears)

The Crew and Passenger Registration Lists of the Seven Acadian Expeditions of 1785
Milton and Norma Reider (1965)

Census of Pointe Coupée, 1745
Bill Barron (Cottonport, LA: Polyanthos, 1978)

Census: 1810 - Louisiana
Ronald Jackson (Salt Lake City, Utah: AIS, 1976)

Census: 1810 and 1820
V. 1 - Avoyelles and St. Landry Parishes (1970)
V. 2 - Iberville, Natchitoches, Pointe Coupée, Rapides Parishes (1972)
V. 3 - Ascension, Assumption, West Baton Rouge, East Baton Rouge, St. Bernard, St. Charles, St. James, St. John the Baptist Parishes (New Orleans: Polyanthos, 1977)
Robert Bruce Ardoin (V. 1 & 2 - Baltimore, MD: Genealogical Publishing Company)

Census: 1820 - Louisiana
Ronald Jackson (Salt Lake City, Utah: AIS, 1976)

Census: 1830 - Louisiana
Ronald Jackson (Salt Lake City, Utah: AIS, 1981)

Census: 1840 - Louisiana
Ronald Jackson (Salt Lake City, Utah: AIS, 1976)

Census: 1840 - Terrebonne Parish
  Phoebe Chauvin Morrison

Census: 1850 - Louisiana
  Ronald Jackson (Salt Lake City, Utah: AIS, 1976)

Census: 1850 - Calcasieu Parish
  Geneva Bailey Seymour (Hebert Publ., 1980: also 1982)

Census: 1850 - Lafourche Parish
  Audrey Westerman (Thibodaux, LA: NSU Library, 1979)

Census: 1850 - St. James Parish
  Elton Oubre (Thibodaux, LA: NSU Library, 1983)

Census: 1850 - Vermilion Parish
  L. Harvey Adams

Census: 1850 - St. John the Baptist Parish
  Michael Maurin (Destrehan, LA: German-Acadian Coast
    Historical & Genealogical Society, 1983)

Census: 1850 - Terrebonne Parish
  Terrebonne Parish Genealogical Society (1985)

Census: 1860 - Louisiana
  Ronald Jackson (Salt Lake City, Utah: AIS)

Census: 1860 - Ascension Parish
  Audrey Westerman (Thibodaux, LA: 1983)

Census: 1860 - Assumption Parish
  Audrey Westerman (Thibodaux, LA: 1983)

Census: 1860 - Calcasieu Parish
  Geneva Bailey Seymour (Hebert Publications: 1980)

Census: 1860 - Lafourche Parish
  Kenneth Toups and June Foret (Toups Enterprises, 1986)

Census: 1860 - St. James Parish
　　Elton Oubre (NSU, 1983)

Census: 1860 - St. Mary Parish
　　Lynda Businelle (Thibodaux, LA: Audrey Westerman, 1986)

Census: 1860 - Terrebonne Parish
　　Terrebonne Genealogical Society (Houma, LA: 1983)

Census: 1860 - Slave Inhabitants of Terrebonne Parish
　　Phillip Chauvin, Jr. (Houma, LA: Terrebonne Genealogical
　　Society, 1985)

Census: 1860 - Vermilion Parish
　　L. Harvey Adams (1973)

Census: 1870 - Louisiana
　　Ronald Jackson (Salt Lake City, Utah: AIS, 1987)

Census: 1870 - Calcasieu Parish
　　Geneva Bailey Seymour (1982)

Census: 1870 - Terrebonne Parish
　　Terrebonne Genealogical Society (Houma, LA: 1985)

Census: 1870 - Assumption Parish
　　Terrebonne Genealogical Society (Houma, LA: 1985)

Census: 1870 - St. Bernard Parish
　　Deborah Donnelly (St. Bernard Genealogical Society: 1984)

Census: 1878 - Iberville Parish Census
　　Judy Riffel (Le Comité de Archives de la Louisiane: 1991)

Census: 1890 - Ascension Parish
　　Rita Babin Butler (Oracle Press, 1983)

Census: 1900 - Terrebonne Parish

Wilma Boudreaux and Phoebe Chauvin Morrison (Thibodaux, LA: Audrey Westerman, 1990)

Census: 1910 - Terrebonne Parish
Terrebonne Parish Genealogical Society (Houma, LA: 1983)

Census Tables for the French Colony of Louisiana, 1699-1732
Charles Maduell (Baltimore, MD: Genealogical Publishing Company, 1972)

Death Notices, 1867-1954: Assumption Parish
Audrey Westerman (Thibodaux, LA: 1983)

Death Notices from Louisiana Newspapers (2 volumes)
Brenda Mayers and Gloria Kerns (Folk Finders, 1984)

Dictionnaire Généalogique des Familles Canadiennes (French)
Cyprien Tanguay (Montreal: Editions Elysee, 1967 also 1975)

Dictionnaire Généalogique des Familles du Quebec (French)
Rene Jette (Les Presses de l'Universite de Montreal, 1983)

Dictionnaire National des Canadiens-Français, 1608-1760 (3 vol.)
Gabriel Drouin (Montreal: Institut Drouin, 1979)

Diocese of Baton Rouge Catholic Church Records

V. 1 - 1707-1769 (1978)	*V. 7 - 1848-1852* (1986)
V. 2 - 1770-1803 (1980)	*V. 8 - 1853-1857* (1988)
V. 3 - 1804-1819 (1982)	*V. 9 - 1858-1862* (1989)
V. 4 - 1820-1829 (1983)	*V. 10 - 1863-1867* (1990)
V. 5 - 1830-1839 (1984)	*V. 11 - 1868-1870* (1991)
V. 6 - 1840-1847 (1986)	*V. 12 - 1871-1873* (1993)

V. 13 - 1874-1876 (1993)
Catholic Diocese of Baton Rouge

Diocese of New Orleans Sacramental Records

V. 1 - 1718-1750 (1987)	*V. 5 - 1792-1795* (1990)
V. 2 - 1751-1771 (1988)	*V. 6 - 1796-1799* (1991)
V. 3 - 1772-1783 (1989)	*V. 7 - 1800-1803* (1992)

V. 4 - 1784-1791 (1989)
  Archdiocese of New Orleans

Early Settlers on the Delta
  Shirley Chiasson Bourquard (1987)

East Ascension Ancestor Charts (2 volumes)
  East Ascension Genealogical and Historical Society (1986)

Evangeline Parish Marriages and Successions, 1911-1912
  Rita Soileau and Ramona Smith (1980)

Exile Without an End
  Chapman Milling (Columbia, S.C.: Bostick & Thornley, 1943)

Federal Land Grants in the Territory of Orleans and the Delta Parishes
  Charles Maduel (Cottonport, LA: Polyanthos, 1975)

The First Families of Louisiana (2 volumes)
  Glenn Conrad (Baton Rouge, LA: Claitor's, 1970)

The First Families of Louisiana, an Index
  Donna Rachal Mills (Mills Historical Press, 1992)

First Settlers of the Louisiana Territory (2 volumes)
  Carolyn Ericson and Frances Ingmire (Ericson Books, 1983)

First Settlers of Pointe Coupée
  Winston De Ville (Cottonport, LA: Polyanthos, 1974)

Generations . . . Past to Present (2 volumes)
  Phoebe Chauvin Morrison (Houma, LA: Terrebonne Genealogical
    Society, 1983)

*The German Coast: Abstracts of the Civil Records of St. Charles and St.
  John the Baptist Parishes, 1804-1812*
  Glenn Conrad (Lafayette, LA: Center for LA Studies, 1981)

The German Coast During the Colonial Era, 1722-1803

Helmut Blume (Destrehan, LA: German-Acadian Coast Historical and
Genealogical Society, 1990)

German "Pest Ships"
Alice Daly Forsyth (New Orleans: Genealogical Research Society of
New Orleans, 1969)

Gulf Coast Colonials
Winston De Ville (Baltimore, MD: Genealogical Publishing Company,
1968)

Le Grande Arrangement des Acadiens au Quebec (8 vol.: French)
Adrien Bergeron (Montreal: Editions Elysee, 1981)

Histoire du Cap-Sable (5 volumes: French)
Clarence Joseph D'Entremont (Hebert Publications, 1981)

Histoire et Genealogie des Acadiens (French)
V. 1 - History of the Acadians (also available in English)
V. 2 - Port Royal
V. 3 - Beaubassin, Grand Pre
V. 4 - Pisiguit, Cobequid, Chipoudy et Petitcoudiac, Cap de
Sable et Pobomcoup, Riviere St. Jean, Ristigouche
V. 5 - Plaisance, Ile Royale, Ile St. Jean
V. 6 - Iles St. Pierre et Miquelon, Iles de la Madeleine,
Bordeaux, Belle Ile en Mer, Louisiana
Bona Arsenault (Ottawa: Editions Lemeac, 1978)

Houma Newspaper Deaths, 1855-1981
Phillip Chauvin, Jr. (Houma, LA: Terrebonne Genealogical Society,
1988)

Iberville Parish Cemeteries
Judy Riffel (Baton Rouge, LA: Le Comité des Archives de la
Louisiane, 1989)

Iberville Parish Records (2 volumes)
Judy Riffel (Baton Rouge, LA: VAAPR, Inc., 1982)

Index to the Archives of Spanish West Florida, 1782-1810
   Stanley Arthur (Cottonport, LA: Polyanthos, 1975)

*Index to the Dispatches of the Spanish Governors of Louisiana,
1766-1792*
   Stanley Arthur (Cottonport, LA: Polyanthos)

Les Idomtes
   Simone Vincens (Rayne, LA: Hebert Publications)

Lafayette Parish Marriage Records, 1823-1830
   Harold Prejean, Jr. (Baton Rouge, LA: VAAPR, Inc., 1984)

The Lafourche Country
   Philip Uzee (Lafayette, LA: Center for LA Studies, 1985)

*Land Holders of Southwest Louisiana: Tax Lists for St. Landry Parish,
1817 and 1818*
   Ramona A. Smith

*The Loppinet Papers, 1687-1710: Genealogical Abstracts of the Earliest
Notarial Records for the Province of Acadia*
   Winston De Ville (Ville Platta, LA: Smith Books, 1991)

Louisiana Census and Militia Lists, 1770-1789
   Albert Robichaux (New Orleans: Polyanthos, 1977)

Louisiana Colonials
   Winston De Ville (1963)

Louisiana in the War of 1812
   Powell Casey (1963)

Louisiana Genealogical Proceedings
   (1960 ->)

Louisiana Marriage Contracts (2 volumes)
   Alice Daly Forsyth (New Orleans: Polyanthos, 1980)

Louisiana Marriages, 1784-1806
  Alice Daly Forsyth (New Orleans: Polyanthos, 1977)

Louisiana Recruits, 1752-1758
  Winston De Ville (Cottonport, LA: Polyanthos, 1973)

Louisiana Soldiers in the War of 1812
  Marion Pierson (Baton Rouge, LA: Louisiana Genealogical and
  Historical Society, 1963)

Louisiana Troops, 1720-1770
  Winston De Ville (American Ref. Publ., 1965)

Louisiana Volunteers in the War of 1898
  Nancy Wright and Cathy Shannon (Houma, LA: 1989)

Les Mariages Acadiens du Quebec (French)
  Albert LeDoux (1981)

Marriage Contracts of the Opelousas Post, 1760-1803
  Jacqueline Vidrine (1960)

*Marriage Contracts, Wills, and Testaments: Spanish Colonial
  Period, 1770-1804*
  Charles Maduell (1969)

Marriage Contracts of the Attakapas Post, 1760-1803
  Winston De Ville (Attakapas Historical Association, 1966)

*Marriage despensations in the Diocese of Louisiana and the
  Floridas, 1786-1803*
  Shirley Chiasson Bourquard (New Orleans: Polyanthos, 1980)

Marriage and Family Relationships of New Orleans, 1830-1840
  Charles Maduell (Baton Rouge, LA: Claitor's, 1984)

Marriages of Jefferson Parish, Louisiana: 1833-1912
  Bartly Bowers (1991)

Memorial to Chênière Caminada
    Terrebonne Genealogical Society (1992)

Mortality Schedule - Louisiana 1850
    Ronald Jackson (Salt Lake City, Utah: AIS, 1979)

The New Orleans French, 1720-1733
    Winston De Ville (Baltimore, MD: Genealogical Publishing Company,
        1973)

New Orleans Ship Lists
    V. 1 - 1820-1821
    V. 2 - 1821-1823
    Milton and Norma Reider (1968)

Notarial Acts of Estevan de Quinones
    V. 1 - 1778-1784 (1964)
    V. 2 - 1785-1786 (1966)
    Elizabeth Gianelloni

Old Families of Louisiana
    Stanley Arthur (New Orleans: Harmanson, 1931)

Old Louisiana Plantation Homes and Family Trees
    Herman Seebold (New Orleans: Pelican Press, 1941)

The Opelousas Post, 1776-1806
    Gladys de Villier (Cottonport, LA: Polyanthos, 1972)

Opelousas Post, 1764-1789
    Jacqueline Vidrine (Baton Rouge, LA: Le Comité des Archives de la
        Louisiane, 1979)

Origine des Familles Canadiennes-Françaises (French)
    Archange Godbout (Societe Saint-Augustin, 1925)

Les Origines Françaises de Premieres Familles Acadiennes (French)
    Nicole T. Bujold (Poiters: Imprimerie l'union, 1979)

Our French-Canadian Ancestors (16 volumes)
    Thomas Laforest (Lisi Press, 1983 ->)

Our Lady of Prompt Succor Cemetery, Chackbay, LA
    Beverly Benoit (1992)

Les Parlers Français d'Acadie (French)
    Genevieve Massignon (Librarie C. Klinsksieck, 1962)

Pintado Papers (on microfilm)

Pioneers of Calcasieu Parish: V. 1 and V. 2
    Nola Mae Wittler Ross (1992)

Pioneers of Calcasieu and Cameron Parish: V. 3
    Nola Mae Wittler Ross (1992)

Pioneers: Terrebonne Parish
    Phoebe Chauvin Morrison (Houma, LA: Terrebonne Genealogical
        Society, 1984)

Post of Avoyelles, 1796-1800
    Winston De Ville (Baton Rouge, LA: Claitor's, 1962)

Post of Pointe Coupée, 1736-1803
    Winston De Ville (Baton Rouge, LA: Claitor's, 1962)

Post Office Records, 1832-1900 (6 volumes)
    Donna Adams

Rapides Post, 1799
    Winston De Ville (Baltimore, MD: Genealogical Publishing
        Company, 1968)

*Rapides Post on Red River: Census and Military Documents for Central
Louisiana, 1769-1800*
    Winston De Ville (1985)

Records of Attakapas District
  V. 1 - St. Martin, 1739-1811
  V. 2 - St. Mary, 1811-1860
  V. 3 - St. Martin, 1808-1860
    Mary Elizabeth Sanders

Records of Louisiana Confederate Soldiers (3 volumes)
    Andrew B. Booth (Spartanburg, S.C.: Reprint Co., 1984)

Rustico: Une Paroisse Acadienne de l'ile du Prince-Edouard
    J-Henri Blanchard

Selected Acadian and Louisiana Church Records (2 volumes)
    George A. Bodin (St. Martinville, LA: Attakapas Historical
      Association, 1968 & 1970)

Settlement of the German Coast in Louisiana
    J. Hanno Deiler (Philadelphia: Americana Germanica Press, 1909: also
      Balt., MD: Genealogical Publ. Co., 1969)

Some Early Families of Avoyelles Parish, Louisiana
    William and Loucille Gremillion (1983)

Some Late 18th Century Louisianians: Census Records, 1758-1796
    Jacqueline Voorhies (Lafayette, LA: USL, 1973)

South Louisiana Records (12 volumes)
  V. 1 - 1794-1840 (1978)   *V. 7 - 1881-1885* (1981)
  V. 2 - 1841-1850 (1978)   *V. 8 - 1886-1890* (1982)
  V. 3 - 1851-1860 (1979)   *V. 9 - 1891-1895* (1982)
  V. 4 - 1861-1870 (1979)   *V. 10 - 1896-1899* (1982)
  V. 5 - 1871-1875 (1981)   *V. 11 - 1900-1902* (1983)
  V. 6 - 1876-1880 (1881)   *V. 12 - Misc. Records* (1985)
    Donald J. Hebert (Hebert Publications)

South Louisiana Vital Family Records (5 volumes)
  V. 1 - 1902-1905 (1984)   *V. 4 - 1914-1917* (1987)
  V. 2 - 1906-1909 (1986)   *V. 5 - 1918-1920* (1988)
  V. 3 - 1910-1913 (1987)

Terrebonne Genealogical Society (Houma, LA)

Southwest Louisiana Records

V. 1 - 1756-1810	*V. 10 - 1871-1872*
V. 2 - 1811-1830	*V. 11 - 1873-1874*
V. 3 - 1831-1840	*V. 12 - 1875-1876*
V. 4 - 1841-1847	*V. 13 - 1877-1878*
V. 5 - 1848-1854	*V. 14 - 1879-1880*
V. 6 - 1855-1860	*V. 15 - 1881-1882*
V. 7 - 1861-1865	*V. 16 - 1883-1884*
V. 8 - 1866-1868	*V. 17 - 1885-1886*
V. 9 - 1869-1870	

V. 18 through 31 cover one year each

V. 32 - 1901 & 1902 Partial
V. 33 - Supplement
V. 34 - 1901 & 1902 Partial
V. 35 - 1903
V. 36 - 1904
 Donald J. Hebert (Hebert Publications, 1974 ->)

The Sainte Catherine Colonists, 1719-1720
 Winston De Ville (1991)

St. Ann Church and Cemetery: Bourg, LA
 Elsie LeJeune

St. Charles: Abstracts of the Civil Records of St. Charles Parish, 1700-1803
 Glenn R. Conrad (Lafayette, LA: History Series, USL, 1974)

St. Francis de Sales Cemetery, Houma
 Pat Barber (Houma, LA: Terrebonne Genealogical Society, 1986)

St. Gabriel Settlers: 1777 Census of Iberville District of Louisiana
 Winston De Ville (1987)

St. James Parish - Colonial Records, 1782-1787

Eileen Behrman (Cut & Shoot, TX: The Clan McBean)

St. Jean Baptiste des Allemands: Abstracts of the Civil Records
of St. John the Baptist Parish
   Glenn R. Conrad (Lafayette, LA: USL, 1982)

St. John the Baptist Cemeteries
   West Baton Rouge Genealogical Society

St. Joseph Cemetery, Lafourche Parish
   Terrebonne Genealogical Society (Houma, LA 1989)

Ship Passenger Lists of the South, 1538-1825
   Carl Boyer (1979)

Sleeping by the Bayous: Cemeteries in the Houma Area
   Billie Robertson (Thibodaux, LA: NSU, 1982)

200 Family Trees, 1590-1981 (6 volumes)
   Youville Laborte (1979-1984)

They Came, They Stayed: Origins of Pointe-aux-Chênes and Ile à Jean
   Charles, 1572-1982
   Laise Marie Ledet (1982)

La Tragédie d'un Peuple (French)
   Emile Lauvrière (Paris: Editions Bossard, 1922)

Vacherie, St. James Parish: History and Genealogy
   Elton Oubre (Thibodaux, LA: Oubre's Books, 1986)

Le Vieux Cimetiere: The Old Ville Platte, LA Cemetery, 1852-1990
   Ramona A. Smith and Kathleen M. Stugg (1991)

Your Ancient Canadian Family Ties
   Reginald Olivier (Logan, Utah: Everton Publishers, 1972)

BACKGROUND MATERIAL

Acadia
Edouard Richard (Home Book Company, 1989 - reprint)

Acadia
Andrew Clark Hill (Madison, Wisconsin: University of Wisconsin Press, 1968)

Acadia and Novia Scotia
Thomas Akins (Cottonport, LA: Polyanthos, 1972)

Acadian Exiles in Pennsylvania
Rene Babineau (1984)

The Acadian Exiles, or French Neutrals in Pennsylvania
William Reed (1858)

Acadian to Cajun: Transformation of a People, 1803-1877
Carl A. Brasseaux (Jackson, MS: University Press of Miss., 1992)

The Acadians in Louisiana Today
Joel Fletcher (Lafayette, LA: 1959)

Acadian Miracle
Dudley LeBlanc (Lafayette, LA: Evangeline Publ. Co., 1966)

The Acadians: Creation of a People
Naomi Griffiths (McGraw-Hill Ryerson Limited, 1973)

The Acadians of Belle Ile en Mer
N.E.S. Griffiths

The Acadians of the Maritimes
Jean Daigle (Minister of the Environment, 1982)

The Acadians of Nova Scotia, Past and Present
Sally Ross and Alphonse Deveau
(Halifax, N.S.: Nimbus Publications, 1992)

Acadian Odyssey
  Oscar Winzerling (Baton Rouge, LA: LSU Press, 1955)

Acadian Reminiscences
  Felix Voorhies (Opelousas, LA: Jacobs News Depot Co., 1907)

Beloved Acadia of My Ancestor
  Yvon Leger (1992)

Cajun Country
  Barry Jean Ancelet, Jay Edwards, and Glen Pitre
    (Jackson, MS: University Press of Mississippi, 1991)

The Cajuns: Essays on Their History and Culture
  Glenn Conrad (Lafayette, LA: Center for LA Studies, 1978)

Catholic Church in Louisiana
  Robert Baudier (New Orleans: A.W. Hyatt, 1939)

The Diocese of Louisiana
  Herman Duncan (New Orleans: A.W. Hyatt, 1888)

The Founding of New Acadia
  Carl Brasseaux (Baton Rouge, LA: LSU Press, 1987)

A Guide to Spanish Louisiana, 1762-1806
  Jack Holmes (New Orleans: A.F. Laborde, 1970)

Early American Series: Early Louisiana, V. 1 - 1700-1819
  Ronald Jackson (AIS, 1981)

French Neutrals in Massachusetts
  Pierre Belliveau (Giffen, 1972)

History of the Acadians
  Bona Arsenault (Le Conseil de la vie francaise en Amerique, 1966)

History of Prince Edward Island

Duncan Campbell (Bowie, MD: Heritage Books)

An Historical Sketch of the Acadians
George Bible (Philadelphia: Ferris and Leach, 1906)

Histoire de la Survivance Acadienne, 1755-1935 (French)
Antoine Bernard (Montreal: Les Clercs de Saint-Viateur, 1935)

Je M'Appelle, A Guide to Pronounciation of Local Names
Edith Hebert (1980)

Life in Acadia
Stan Garrod and Rosemary Neering

The People Called Cajuns
James Dorman (Lafayette, LA: Center for LA Studies, 1983)

"Scattered to the Wind": Dispersal and Wanderings of the Aadians, 1755-1809
Carl A. Brasseaux (Lafayette, LA: Center for Louisiana Studies, 1991)

The Story of the Acadians
Amy Boudreau (New Orleans: Pelican Publ., 1955)

True Story of the Acadians
Dudley LeBlanc (Lafayette, LA: 1932)

Xplorin' Acadians
Sherwin Guidry (1984)

REFERENCE

Acadian-Cajun Genealogical Periodical Article Index
Timothy Hebert (P.O. Box 1416, Houma, LA, 70361: 1990)

The Archives
Loretta D. Szucs and Sandra Luebking (Salt Lake City, Utah: Ancestry Publ., 1988)

Bayouland Genealogical Resources Catalog
   Bayouland Library System (Lafayette, LA: 1985)

Corrections to Arsenault's Histoire et Genealogie des Acadiens
   Janet Jehn (Kentucky: Acadian Genealogy Exchange, 1988)

County Courthouse Book
   Genealogy Publishing Company (1990)

The Courthouses of Louisiana
   Carl Brasseaux (Lafayette, LA: Center for LA Studies, 1977)

Directory of American Libraries with Genealogical or Local
 History Collections
   P. William Filby (Wilmington, DE: Scholarly Resources, 1988)

Directory of Family Associations
   Elizabeth Petty Bentley (Baltimore, MD: Genealogical Publications
      Co.)

Genealogical Materials in the New Orleans Public Library
   Collin Hamer (New Orleans: Friends of the New Orleans Public
      Library, 1984)

Genealogical Research and Resources
   Lois Gilmer (American Library Association, 1988)

Genealogical Research in Nova Scotia
   Terrence M. Punch (Halifax, N.S.: Petheric Press, 1978)

The Genealogist's Address Book
   Elizabeth Bentley (Baltimore, MD: Genealogy Publ. Co., 1992)

Genealogist's Handbook for Atlantic Canada Research
   Terrence M. Punch (Boston: New England Historical and
      Genealogical Society, 1989)

A Guide to Archival Material Held by the Catholic Diocese of

Baton Rouge
Elisabeth Doyle (Baton Rouge, LA: 1964)

A Guide to Church Records in Louisiana, 1720-1975
Donald J. Hebert (Hebert Publications, 1975)

A Guide to the History of Louisiana
L.T. Cummins and G. Jeansonne (Westport, Connecticut: Greenwood
Press, 1982)

*Guide to Printed Sources for Genealogical and Historical Research in the
Louisiana Parishes*
Yvette Boling (Baton Rouge, LA: Louisiana Genealogical and
Historical Society, 1985)

How to Publish and Market Your Family History
Carl Boyer (1982)

How to Write the Story of Your Family
Nola Mae Wittler Ross (1992)

In Search of Your Canadian Roots
Angus Baxter

In Search of Your Roots: A Guide for Canadians Seeking Their Ancestors
Angus Baxter (Toronto: Macmillan of Canada, 1978)

Inventaire General des Sources Documentaires Sur les Acadiens
(3 volumes: French)
Centre d'Etudes Acadiennes (Moncton: Editions d'Acadie, 1975-1977)

Inventories of Parish Archives for various parishes
W.P.A.

An Index of New Orleans Confirmations, 1789-1841
Donald J. Hebert (Baton Rouge, LA: Claitor's, 1984)

An Index of Old Cemetery and Church Records in Louisiana
National Society of the Colonial Dames of America (1972)

Index and Key Words to Histoire et Genealogie des Acadiens
    Donald J. Hebert (Hebert Publications, 1979)

Index to Bona Arsenault's Histoire et Genealogie des Acadiens
    Phoebe Chauvin Morrison (1990)

Introduction to Family Research
    Shirley Chiasson Bourquard (St. Bernard Genealogical Society, 1980)

The Library
    Johni Cerny and Wendy Elliott (Salt Lake City, Utah: Ancestry
        Publishing, 1988)

The Library of Congress
    James C. Neagles (Salt Lake City, Utah: Ancestry Publ., 1990)

Louisiana Surname Index
    Nicholas Murray (Hammond, LA: Hunting for Bears, 1984)

Publishing Short-Run Books
    Dan Poynter (Santa Barbara, CA: Para Publishing, 1987)

The Researcher's Guide to Louisiana Genealogy
    (Gretna, LA: Heritage Publishing Co., 1980)

Researching Acadian Families
    Donald J. Hebert (Hebert Publications)

Researching Your Ancestors in New Brunswick, Canada
    Robert Fellows (Toronto: Public Archives of N.B., 1979)

*A Selected Bibliography of Acadian History, Culture, and Genealogy, 1955-
    1985*
        Carl Brasseaux (Thibodaux, LA: Ellender Memorial Library,
            NSU, 1985)

The Source
    Arlene Eakle and Johni Cerny (Salt Lake City, Utah: Ancestry

Publishing, 1984)

A Southern Catholic Heritage
Charles Nolan (Archdiocese of New Orleans, 1976)

Sources of Spanish Records in Louisiana
Pearl Segura (Baton Rouge, LA: Louisiana Genealogical and Historical
Society, 1961)

Tracing Your Ancestors in Nova Scotia
Julie Morris (Halifax, N.S.: Public Archives of N.S., 1981)

Tracing Your Civil War Ancestors
Bertram Groene (1973)

Who's Who in Acadian Genealogical Research, V. 2
Peter Gallant Berlo (1992)

FAMILY BOOKS
(Alphabetical by family name)

The Alberts of Lafourche
Linzy Albert (1979)

*Genealogical and Historical Sketch of the Nicolas Albert Family,
1726-1985*
Linzy D. Albert (1985)

The Arseman, Arsement, Arcement Family
Raoul Arcement (Wendy's Printing Service, 1981)

Autin Families: Canada to Louisiana, 1720-1985
Traise W. Hebert (Thibodaux, LA: Audrey Westerman, 1985)

Louisiana Descendants of Simon Aycock, 1760-1976
Albert Aycock (Carlsbad, CA: BOP Printing, 1976)

Babineau

René Babineau (Richibouctou, N.B.: Le Club International des
    Acadiens)

The Benoist d'Etiveaud Story, 1308 to 1973
    Henry Alton Detiveaux

Bernard Family Tree, 1620-1973
    Juanita Bernard

Descendants of Exzelia Elizabeth Bergeron
    Betty Lou Madden (Cornhusker Press, 1982)

Ancestors of Exzelia Elizabeth Bergeron
    Betty Lou Madden (Cornhusker Press, 1980)

Boudreaux
    Patricia Boudreaux Blanchard (1993)

An Acadian Pedigree (Boudreaux family)
    Cleveland J. Fruge (Baton Rouge, LA: Claitor's, 1972)

Bouchard Genealogy
    Linda Dube

The Genealogy of Antoine Bourg
    Leola Bourg (1978)

La Famille Bourg-Bourque de Port Royal, 1609-1969 (French)
    Joan Campbell (Yarmouth, N.S.: Les Editions Lescarbot, 1972)

Genealogy of the Bourgeois Family
    Helen Carvin (Belford, N.J.: E.A. Carvin, 1983)

Bourgeois Lines
    Kenneth Toups (Thibodaux, LA: Audrey Westerman, 1985)

A Breaux Family History
    Gerald Breaux (Fort Worth, TX: 1980)

The Ancestry of Certain Breaux, Broussard, Louviere, Barras, Bonin,
Provost, and Guilbeau Families of Louisiana, Acadie, Quebec, and France
  Clarence T. Breaux

The Acadian Breaux's of Louisiana
  Gustave Breaux (Fort Worth, TX: 1980)

Chauvin dit Charleville
  Elizabeth Shown Mills (Mississippi State University, 1976)

The Descending Families of Louis Chauvin and His Three Wives
  Phoebe Chauvin Morrison (Thib., LA: Audrey Westerman, 1986)

The Descending Families of Zenon Chauvin
  Phoebe Chauvin Morrison (Thib., LA: Audrey Westerman, 1991)

The Book of Clouatre
  Nora Clouatre Pollard (1974)

The Daigle Family
  Ethel T. Daigle (1991)

The Daigle Family—Acadia to Valence
  Ethel Tregre Daigle (1991)

D'Aspit de Saint-Amand: French Roots
  Michael Bergeron

Domingue of Louisiana
  Edward J. Domangue (1991)

La Famille Comeau de la Baie Sainte-Marie
  J. Alphonse Deveau

Edelmayer
  Elton Oubre (New Orleans: Genealogical Research Society of New
    Orleans, 1984)

Falgoust History and Genealogy

Barbara Allen (1988)

Louisiana Fontenot
Bruce Ardoin (Evangeline Genealogical and Historical Society, 1984)

The Fortier Family and Allied Families
G'Nell F. McKenzie (1992)

The Fruges of Fakaitaic
J. Cleveland Fruge (Baton Rouge, LA: Claitor's, 1971)

Gaudet Family in North America: A Lineage
Charles A. Gaudet (1992)

La Famille Girouard (French)
Desire Girouard (Dorval, 1884)

Granger
Geneva Seymour (1981)

Some of the Descendants of Etienne Hebert
Purvis Hebert (Mililani Town, Hawaii: 1978)

Hebert of Hecker
Geneva Seymour (1983)

The Hebert Family, Vol. 1
Timothy Hebert (Houma, LA: 1993)

L'Arbe Généalogique du les Landrys
Linda Landry Woolford

Grandpa with a Stick: Joseph Theslin Landry
Norma Pontiff Evans (1980)

Landry-Gassie: Another Louisiana Family Genealogy
J. Cleveland Fruge (1975)

The Book of LeBlanc

Nora Pollard (Baton Rouge, LA: Claitor's, 1973)

Des Ledets de la Louisiane
E.J. Ledet (1986)

The Lejeunes of Acadia and the Youngs of Southwest Louisiana
John A. Young (Basile, LA: 1991)

Marchands on the Mississippi
Sidney Marchand (1968)

The Martin Family
Dana Martin (Thibodaux, LA: Audrey Westerman, 1986)

The Moutons
J. Franklin Mouton (1978)

The Line of Descendants of the Family of Jean Mouton
Grover Mouton (Crowley, LA: 196?)

Pontiff Paths
Norma Pontiff Evans (1982)

Descendants of Jean Rodrigue and Anne LeRoy
Wilma Boudreaux and Sandra Henry (1990)

Les Savoie: Une grande famille acadienne au Nouveau-Brunswick
Fidèle Theriault (1992)

Savoy Heritage: 1621 to the Present
Louis Savoy (Smithtown, N.Y.: Exposition Press, 1983)

Savoy Savoie Savois Families
Harry Savoy (1987)

Cajun Roots: The Genealogy of Joseph Octave Theriot and Viola Broussard
Beverly Theriot Coleman (Lake Charles, LA: Andrus, 1982)

Gustave Thibodeaux Generations: Past to Present
    Alvenia Thibodeaux (1984)

The Gilbert Thibodeaux Family
    Claire Thibodeaux (1975)

The Toups Clan and How It All Began
    Neil Toups (Neilson, 1969)

Trahan, VI: Nicolas to Guillaume to You
    Mitch Conover (1992)

A Trahan History
    Conrad Trahan (1979)

Vidrine-Vedrines
    Jacqueline Olivier Vidrine (Lafayette, LA: Acadiana Press, USL, 1981)

Zerangue, Zeringue, Zyrangue and Allied Families
    Agnes Foreman (Baltimore, MD: Gateway Press, 1979)

APPENDIX E

THE HISTORY OF ACADIANS AND CAJUNS

ACADIAN HISTORY

Although the New World was discovered by Europeans around 1000, no real attempts at settlement were made until the sixteenth century. In the early seventeenth century, France attempted one of its first settlements in what is now the Canadian Maritime Provinces. A group of settlers landed on St. Croix Island in 1604. The next year they moved to Acadia (now called Nova Scotia). In 1605, the town of Port Royal was founded. Only male settlers inhabited the town for the first 30+ years. They were often faced with attacks from the English. England and France would be at war off and on throughout the next hundred and sixty years, and the Acadians would be in the middle of things. In 1632, the Treaty of St. Germain-en-Laye brought peace to the area.

The *St. Jehan* arrived in Acadia in 1636. Three of these settlers would leave descendants in Acadia. Shortly after, more settlers arrived from France. They settled in and adjusted to their new home. New French settlers would continue to arrive sporadically over the next half century.

Then, in 1655, English hostilities started again and continued until the Treaty of Breda in 1670. Once again, a period of peace allowed the Acadians to grow and prosper. In 1690, the English again captured Port Royal. Hostilities ended for a while with the Treaty of Ryswick in 1697. From 1704 to 1710, the Acadians were besieged again. Finally, in 1710, Port Royal was captured by the English for the last time. The Treaty of Utrecht in 1713 gave permanent possession of Acadia to the English.

Except for the English soldiers, the entire population of the area was Acadian. The English wanted to get rid of the Acadians. England and France were still at odds elsewhere, and the English did not want the Acadians (who were from France) to take up arms against them. But they couldn't afford to lose them. They needed the Acadians to provide them with goods and labor, as there were no English settlers in the area.

It was an uneasy period of time from 1713 to 1755. Acadians were often treated badly and were sometimes forced to work as "slaves". They did go about their lives . . . farming, going to church, and raising families. The population increased by several hundred percent during this period.

They proved to be of no threat to the English. The Acadians wanted no part of the French-English conflicts. They took an oath to remain neutral. In fact, they were called French Neutrals because of their attitude.

In 1749, the English finally managed to settle 2,576 colonists in Acadia. The English wanted their own colonists to supply their needs. Many of the Acadians moved north to Isle St. Jean and Isle Royale to avoid persecution by the English.

In 1755, Lt. Colonel Robert Monckton attacked and captured the French fort at Beausejour. The Acadians there fought against the English. They had no choice, as the French had threatened them with death. Lt. Colonel Monckton understood this and pardoned them. Governor Charles Lawrence, who had long wanted to get rid of the Acadians, used this incident to his advantage. Citing the Acadian participation at Beausejour, he managed to pass a resolution to deport the Acadians. He told the Acadians to take an unconditional oath to England; but, in a private memo, he notes that he will deport them even if they take the oath.

Starting in October, 1755, the English began rounding up the Acadians and deporting them to the American colonies. The destinations are as follows.

2000 to Massachusetts	900 to Maryland
1500 to Virginia	450 to Pennsylvania
1027 to South Carolina	450 to Georgia
900 to Connecticut	250 to New York

Those that survived the voyage were often received as outcasts. The Protestant colonists strongly objected to their new Catholic neighbors. The fact that most of the Acadians had no way to support themselves and spoke a foreign language didn't help matters. In Virginia, they weren't even allowed off the boat. Those 1500 Acadians were sent to England to wait in detention centers. When the hostilities between France and England ended in 1763, those Acadians that had survived the ordeal were transported to Morlaix, France.

After the initial deportations in 1755, there were still thousands of Acadians in the Nova Scotia area. Most of them were moving to Isle St. Jean, Isle Royale, and New Brunswick. In 1758, the last French stronghold, Louisbourg, was taken by the English. The French troops stationed there were sent to England. The wounded officers and inhabitants of Louisbourg were sent to France. Also, the entire Acadian population of Isle St. Jean and Isle Royale were to be deported to France.

In 1758, over 2000 Acadians were deported to France from Isle St. Jean. Like the other deportations, it was not an easy trip. Two ships (with 700 people) sank on the way. One third of the passengers on the other ships died along the way. Most of these last deportations arrived at St. Malo, France. As they found groups of Acadians over the next five years, the English would have them deported. The deportations stopped in 1763 with the Treaty of Paris.

The deported Acadians who were sent to France arrived at several ports. Some of these ports were St. Malo, La Rochelle, Ile D'Aix, Morlaix, Rochefort, Le Havre, Cherbourg, Calais, Dunkerque, Bordeaux, Brest, Cancale, and Boulogne-en-Mer. Most of the Acadians had been laborers. Without land of their own, they were dependent upon the government for support.

Once in France, the Acadians congregated in two main areas: Ille-et-Vilaine and Cotes-du-Nord. They were trying to find relatives separated from them during the deportation and wanted to be with "their people." Though the original Acadian settlers were French, some of these Acadians had been in the New World for six generations. France was a "foreign" country to them. Ninety-eight percent of the Acadians in France were at these two areas by 1762.

Across the Atlantic Ocean, the Acadians in the American colonies tried to manage as best they could, but were generally treated poorly. Some made their way back to Acadia, only to be deported again. Some went to Canada to join other Acadians who had fled there. Overland travel was difficult because France and England were at war until 1763. No concrete evidence of Acadians in Louisiana exists until 1764, when the first few church records of Acadians begin to appear.

Over the next two decades, as other Acadians in the colonies found out about the successful settlement in Louisiana, the Acadian population there grew. The population of Acadians in Louisiana had reached over 1000 by 1785. One of the main settlement areas was the Attakapas District in south-central Louisiana. This area was centered around the town of St. Martinville. Another popular place was the Acadian Coast. This area was in the present-day parishes of Ascension and St. James. The Spanish government had the Acadians settle there to provide a "buffer zone", as the English controlled the land just north of the area. Some of the Acadian Coast residents gradually moved down Bayou Lafourche.

Meanwhile, the Acadians in France were still trying to find a home. They did not like living on "welfare." In 1764, 24 Acadian families from Morlaix went to Cayenne in South America. Many Acadians who had arrived from St. Pierre and Miquelon in 1766-1768 went back at the end of 1768 (although they were sent back to France in 1778).

The French government wanted to get the Acadian families on their own and tried setting up a couple of settlements for them. In 1765, the government moved 78 Acadian families (55 from Morlaix, 22 from St. Malo, and 1 from Boulogne) to Belle-Isle-en-Mer. But the land was infertile and the settlement failed.

A census was taken in 1773 to determine the population of the Acadians in France. The census results are as follows.

LOCATION	NUMBER OF FAMILIES	NUMBER OF PEOPLE
St. Malo	425	1712
Cherbourg	60	222
At harbors	56	167
Morlaix	45	166
Rochefort	27	69
La Rochelle	9	26
Nantes	3	7
Dunkerque	1	1
Total	626	2370

Almost two-thirds of the population was composed of laborers and those in agricultural trades. These were the people that needed a place to settle down. The craftsmen could support their families at the port cities. In 1774, a major settlement was attempted inland at Poitou. When the crops failed to yield a harvest in 1774 and 1775, the settlement was declared a failure. The Acadians (1,369 of them) went from Chatellerault to Nantes in four convoys. They remained in that area, being supported by the government, until 1785.

A Frenchman named Peroux who had traveled to Louisiana brought back stories of the successful settlement of the Acadians in that territory (which was now under Spain's control). As a result of efforts led by Peroux, King Charles III of Spain agreed to pay to transport the Acadians to

Louisiana. Almost all of the Acadians at Nantes wanted to go. A much smaller percentage at St. Malo were interested in the trip.

In 1785, seven ships departed France for Louisiana. A listing of these ships and the number of passengers on each is found below.

SHIP	NUMBER OF FAMILIES	NUMBER OF PEOPLE
Le Bon Papa	34	156
La Bergere	72	267
Le Beaumont	45	178
Le St. Remi	79	336
L'Amitie	78	291
La Ville d'Archangel	54	330
La Caroline	25	75

Many of these people were settled along the west bank of the Mississippi from upper Iberville Parish to lower Pointe Coupée, but most of the passengers settled in the Lafourche area. A few settled at Bayou des Ecores above Baton Rouge, but later moved down to Lafourche when a hurricane wiped out the settlement in 1794.

Though several cultures were already in Louisiana when the Acadians arrived, the Acadian way of life clearly dominated the places in which they settled. Certain items were borrowed from other cultures, but they all fit together under the term "Cajun".

LOUISIANA HISTORY

As mentioned above, several other nationalities combined with the Acadians to form the Cajun culture. These nationalities include Germans, French, French-Canadians, Spanish, English, blacks, and Native Americans.

The first of this group to settle Louisiana at the beginning of the 1700s was the French. The first settlers were military personnel, trappers, and fortune-seekers. French settlers continued to enter Louisiana for the rest of the century. Most of them remained around New Orleans, although some ventured out and mixed in with the surrounding population.

The French-Canadians, French settlers who had earlier colonized Canada, moved into Louisiana shortly after the arrivals from France. Since Louisiana was owned by France (for most of the century), they could be with other Frenchmen. France also encouraged them to move to Louisiana. Since the Canadian settlements had been around since the early 1600s, the Canadians would be more experienced at settling a New World colony.

The Germans began arriving in 1721. They came to the New World under the John Law concession to settle in Arkansas. When the arrangements fell through, they decided to settle along the Mississippi River above New Orleans. This settlement in St. Charles Parish was called the German Coast. It later expanded along the river to St. John the Baptist Parish, and a second German Coast was formed. Though they were Protestant, they soon adapted to the Catholic way of life. By the end of the eighteenth century, some of them had moved away from the River . . . and other nationalities had moved into their community. Other Germans came in the 1800s, but not in a single group. Many of these settled in urban areas, though some made their way into Cajun country.

Spain, which controlled Louisiana for most of the latter half of the eighteenth century, did not try a major settling of their people. Of course, some Spaniards did make their way to Louisiana. Many of the military personnel stayed on in Louisiana to settle down. In 1778, a group of Spanish citizens from the Canary Islands came to America. They settled in four major areas: Terre-aux-Bouef area, Valenzuela (Assumption Parish), Galveztown (which failed and was abandoned).

The English didn't really come into the picture until the nineteenth century, after the United States had purchased the Louisiana Territory. Since then, most of the settlers in Louisiana have come from other states; and many of those settlers were English. Some of the early English settlers were wealthy planters. They would buy up land (which the Acadians and others had originally settled) and run large plantation operations.

The major Native American population to mix with the Cajuns was the Houma Indians. Most of the Houma Indians were located in Terrebonne and Lafourche parishes. Their numbers in the late eighteenth century were small compared to the other nationalities.

Of course, many others moved into the area in the nineteenth and twentieth centuries. These included a number of European nationalities and peoples from the islands and nations of the western hemisphere. Thousands of immigrants came to Louisiana from Saint-Domingue at the beginning of the nineteenth century. Large numbers of French (the "Foreign French") and German immigrants came to the United States (and Louisiana) in the 1800s. A large number of Irish made their way to Louisiana in the 1800s. At the end of the nineteenth century, the Italians immigrated in significant numbers. Many of these came to escape oppression or conflicts in their native land. Others came to the United States to achieve their own "American dream." These immigrants blended into the Acadian-Cajun communities.

The Acadian-Cajun way of life entered the twentieth century virtually unchanged, especially in rural areas. It wasn't until transportation, communication, industry, and education improved that their culture began to change.

All of these people came together to form the Cajun people. Today, the people and the culture can still be seen. Twenty-two parishes in south Louisiana are known as the Acadiana area. It is here that the Cajun influence is most strongly felt.

APPENDIX F

ACADIAN-CAJUN TIMELINE

1604 First settlement at St. Croix Island.

1605 Port Royal is settled. Hostilities arise periodically because of English desires on the area.

1632 The Treaty of St. Germain-en-Laye brings an era of peace between the French & English.

1636 The *St. Jehan* arrives with French settlers. More settlers will arrive periodically until the end of the century.

1655 The English capture Port Royal. Hostilities by the English resume.

1670 The Treaty of Breda ends hostilities.

1671 The first Acadian census counts 340 people.

1672 The Acadian community of Beaubassin is founded.

1682 The Acadian community of Grand Pré is founded.

1687 A church is built at Grand Pré.

1690 The English re-capture Port Royal and continue their periodic raids on Acadia.

1697 The Treaty of Ryswick brings peace (for a while).

1701 A census is taken, counting 1,450 Acadians.

1704 Queen Anne's War starts . . . the English attacks resume.

1708 The Acadian community of Petitcodiac is founded.

1708 "The more I consider these people, the more I believe they are the happiest in the world."—by French governor Daniel Subercase.

1710 Port Royal is captured for the last time by the English. It will be renamed Annapolis Royal and will remain in English hands.

1713 The Treaty of Utrecht permanently gives Acadia to the English. But, for over 35 years, the only settlers in Acadia are the Acadians. The Acadians take an oath of neutrality . . . they would fight for neither the French nor the English.

1721 The John Law concession brings German settlers to the New World. Instead of settling in Arkansas, they settle along the Mississippi River above New Orleans (the German Coast).

1749 The English manage to get 2,576 colonial settlers to move to Acadia.

1755 Acadians are forced to fight against the English at Beausejour. Gov. Lawrence uses this to get the Acadians deported. Starting in October, thousands of Acadians are deported to the American colonies. About half of the 16,000 to 20,000 Acadians will ultimately be deported. Many more will leave on their own.

1758 Louisbourg is taken by the English. The Acadians who had fled to Isle Royale and Isle St. Jean are deported to France.

1762 A French census counts 1, 126 Acadians in France.

1763 The Treaty of Paris ends hostilities between France and England. The Acadians who had been held in England are brought to France.

1764 The first Acadian records appear in Louisiana.

1765 Seventy-eight Acadian families try to develop a settlement at Belle-Isle-en-Mer, France, but it fails.

1766 Spain gains control of Louisiana.

1773 A French census counts 2,370 Acadians in France.

1774   Over 1,000 Acadians try to develop a settlement at Poitou, France, but it fails after a couple of years. These Acadians will move to Nantes.

1778   Several shiploads of Spanish settlers from the Canary Islands start arriving.

1785   Spain pays for seven ships to take Acadians to settle in Louisiana. Over 1,500 people make the journey.

1803   The United States buys Louisiana.

1812   Louisiana becomes a state.

APPENDIX G

CANADIAN AND LOUISIANA GENEALOGICAL SOCIETIES AND THEIR PUBLICATIONS

American-Canadian Genealogical Society
P.O. Box 668
Manchester, NH 03105

> Publication: *The Genealogist*
> Membership: $15

Attakapas Historical Association
USL
P.O. Box 43010
Lafayette, LA 70504

> Publication: *The Attakapas Gazette*
> Membership: $10

Baton Rouge Genealogical and Historical Society
P.O. Box 80565
Baton Rouge, LA 70898-0565

> Publication: *Le Baton Rouge*
> Membership: $15

East Ascension Genealogical and Historical Society
P.O. Box 1006
Gonzales, LA 70707-1006

> Publication: *Journal of the East Ascension Genealogical and Historical Society*
> Membership: $10

Evangeline Genealogical and Historical Society
P.O. Box 664
Ville Platte, LA 70586

Publication: *La Voix des Prairies*
Membership: $10

Genealogical Association of Nova Scotia
P.O. Box 641
Station M
Halifax, Nova Scotia B3J 2T3

Publication: *Nova Scotia Genealogist*

Genealogical Research Society of New Orleans
P.O. Box 51791
New Orleans, LA 70151

Publication: *New Orleans Genesis*
Membership: $25

German-Acadian Coast Historical and Genealogical Society
P.O. Box 517
Destrehan, LA 70047

Publication: *Les Voyagers*
Membership: $15

Lafourche Heritage Society
P.O. Box 513
Thibodaux, LA 70302

The Louisiana Genealogical and Historical Society
P.O. Box 3454
Baton Rouge, LA 70821

Publication: *The Louisiana Genealogical Register*
Membership: $15

Le Société des Cajuns
121 West 111 Street
Cutoff, LA 70345

Southwest Louisiana Genealogical Society
P.O. Box 5652
Lake Charles, LA 70606-5652

Publication: *Kinfolks*
Membership: $10

Springfield City Library
220 State St.
Springfield, MA 01103

Publication: *French-Canadian-American Genealogy*

St. Bernard Genealogical Society
P.O. Box 271
Chalmette, LA 70044

Publication: *L'Heritage*
Membership: $17.50

St. Mary Genealogical and Historical Society
P.O. Box 662
Morgan City, LA 70381

Publication: *St. Mary Links*
Membership: $18.50

Terrebonne Genealogical Society
P.O. Box 295
Station 2
Houma, LA 70360

Publication: *Terrebonne Lifelines*
Membership: $20

There are also some periodicals published independently.

Acadian Genealogy Exchange
863 Wayman Branch Road
Covington, KY 41015-2250

    Subscription: $12

The French Canadian-Acadian Genealogical Review
C.P. 845, Upper Town
Ville de Quebec, Quebec
Canada

Le Reveil Acadien
P.O. Box 53
Marlorough, Massachusetts 01752

There are no Acadian genealogical societies in Canada.   There are
several Acadian historical societies. Some of these are listed below.

Société Historique Acadienne de la Baie Saint-Marie
Université Sainte-Anne
Pointe-de-l'Eglise, Nova Scotia B0W 1M0

Société Historique Acadienne
C.P. 2363, Succursale A
Moncton, New Brunswick E1C 8J3

Société Historique Acadienne de l'ile du Prince Edouard
C.P. 88
Summerside, P.E.I. C1N 4P6

APPENDIX H

LIBRARIES WITH SIGNIFICANT ACADIAN-CAJUN RESOURCES

CANADA

Centre d'Etudes Acadiennes
Université de Moncton
Moncton, New Brunswick E1A 3E9

The Center publishes a periodical, *Contact-Acadie.*

National Archives of Canada (613) 995-5138
National Library of Canada
395 Wellington St.
Ottawa, Ontario K1A 0N3
M-F 8:30-4:45

Bibliotheque Nationale du Quebec (514) 873-4553
1700 Rue Saint-Denis
Montreal, Quebec H2X 3K6
T-S 9-5   Summer: M-F 9-5

Ontario Genealogical Society Library (416) 489-0734
North York Public Library
6th Floor
5120 Yonge St.
Toronto, Ontario M2N 5N9
M-Th 9-8:30   F 9-6   S 9-5

PEI Museum & Heritage Foundation (902) 892-9127
2 Kent St.
Charlottetown, Prince Edward Island C1A 1M6

Provincial Archives of New Brunswick (506) 453-2122
P.O. Box 6000
Bonar Law Building
University of New Brunswick Campus

Fredericton, NB E3B 5H1
M-S 8:30-5

Public Archives of Nova Scotia (902) 423-9115
6016 University Avenue
Halifax, Nova Scotia B3H 1W4
M-F 8:30-10   S 9-6   Su 1-10

Annapolis Valley Regional Library (902) 532-2260
Grange St.
Annapolis Royal, Nova Scotia B0S 1AO
NOTE* Regional libraries also exist in:
Amherst, Bridgewater, Dartmouth, Halifax, Mulgrave, New Glasgow,
    Sydney, and Yarmouth

Centre Acadien
Université Saint-Anne
Pointe-de-l'Eglise, Nova Scotia B0W 1M0

OUTSIDE LOUISIANA
Maine State Library   (207) 289-5600
Sta. 64
Cultural Building
Augusta, Maine 04333
M,W,F 9-5   T,Th 9-9   S 11-5

National Archives   (202) 523-3218
Eighth and Pennsylvania Avenue
Washington, D.C. 20408
M-F 8:45-10   S 8:45-5:15

National Archives-Southwest Region (817) 334-5525
501 West Felix Street
Fort Worth, TX 76115
M-F 8-4

Library of Congress   (202) 287-5537
10 First St., S.E.
Washington, D.C. 20540

M-F 8:30-9:30   S 8:30-5   Su 1-5

Family History Library of the
Church of Jesus Christ of
Latter-day Saints   (801) 531-2331
Genealogical Society of Utah
35 North West Temple
Salt Lake City, UT 84150
M 7:30-6   T-F 7:30-10   S 7:30-5

LOUISIANA

There are various amounts of Acadian-Cajun material available at these libraries. As you might expect, the libraries in the larger cities and universities usually have more material. The farther you go from the center of the Acadiana area, the less material you will find. But you will find that most of the parish libraries have all of the important Acadian-Cajun reference books. And there are more that aren't even listed here. Just about any library in south Louisiana will have this type of material. Several of them have publications listing their genealogical holdings:.

University of Southwestern Louisiana (318) 231-6027
Center for Louisiana Studies
Dupre Library
P.O. Box 40831
Lafayette, Louisiana 70804
M-F   7:30-4:30

Louisiana State Library   (504) 342-4914
760 Riverside Mall
Baton Rouge, Louisiana 70821
M-F 8-4:30

Louisiana State Archives   (504) 922-1207
3851 Essen Lane
Baton Rouge, Louisiana 70809
M-F 8-4:30   S 9-5   Su 1-5

Louisiana State Land Office (504) 342-4578
625 North Fourth Street - Rm 1201

625 North Fourth Street - Rm 1201
Baton Rouge, LA 70804
M-F 7:30-4:30

Middleton Library   (504) 388-5652
Louisiana State University
Baton Rouge, LA 70803
M-F 7:15-midnight   S 8-5   Su 12-midnight

Hill Memorial Library   (504) 388-6551
Louisiana State University
Baton Rouge, LA 70803
M-F 9-5   S 9-1

LeDoux Library   (318) 457-7311
Louisiana State University
P.O. Box 1129
Eunice, LA 70535
M-Th 7:30-7   F 7:30-5

New Orleans Public Library (504) 596-2610
219 Loyola Ave.
New Orleans, LA 70140
M-Th, S 10-6

Historic New Orleans Collection (504) 523-4662
533 Royal St.
New Orleans, LA 70130
T-S 10-4:30

Louisiana State Museum   (504) 568-8215
Louisiana Historical Center Library
Old US Mint
400 Esplanade Ave.
New Orleans, LA 70116
W-F 10-4:45

Howard-Tilton Memorial Library (504) 865-5643
Tulane University

M-F 8:30-5   S 10-5

Nicholls State University   (504) 448-4646
Ellender Library
Thibodaux, Louisiana 70310

PARISH LIBRARIES
Acadia Parish   (318) 788-1880
1125 North Parkerson Avenue
P.O. Drawer 1509
Crowley, LA 70526

Ascension Parish   (504) 473-8052
218 Railroad Avenue
P.O. Box 588
Donaldsonville, LA 70346

Assumption Parish   (504) 369-7070
108 Jefferson St.
P.O. Drawer A
Napoleonville, LA 70390
M,W,Th 8:30-5:30   T 8:30-7   S 9-1

East Baton Rouge Parish   (504) 389-3360
7711 Goodwood Blvd.
Baton Rouge, LA 70806

Centroplex Library   (504) 389-4960
120 St. Louis St.
Baton Rouge, LA 70821
M-Th 8-7   F-S 9-6   Su 2-6

Evangeline Parish   (318) 363-1369
242 West Main St.
P.O. Box 40
Ville Platte, LA 70586

Iberia Parish   (318) 367-2584
445 East Main St.

Acadian-Cajun Genealogy

P.O. Box 1089
New Iberia, LA 70560

Iberville Parish   (504) 344-6948
1501 J. Gerald Berret Blvd.
P.O. Box 736
Plaquemine, LA 70764
M 8:30-6   T-Th 8:30-5:30   F 8:30-5

Jefferson Parish   (504) 834-5850
3420 N. Causeway Blvd.
P.O. Box 7490
Metairie, LA 70010
M-F 9-8   S 9-5

Jefferson Davis Parish   (318) 824-1210
526 North Main St.
P.O. Box 356
Jennings, LA 70546

Lafayette Parish   (318) 233-0587
301 W. Congress St.
P.O. Box 3427
Lafayette, LA 70506
Winter: M-Th 9-9   F-S 9-5
Summer: M-W 9-7   Th 9-9   F 9-5   S 9-4

Lafourche Parish   (504) 447-4119
314 St. Mary St.
P.O. Box 998
Thibodaux, LA 70301
M-F 9-6   S 9-5

Plaquemines Parish   (504) 657-7121
203 Louisiana Highway 23, South
Buras, LA 70041

Pointe Coupée Parish   (504) 638-7593
201 Claiborne St.

New Roads, LA 70760

St. Bernard Parish   (504) 279-0448
1125 East St. Bernard Hwy
Chalmette, LA 70043

St. Charles Parish   (504) 785-8464
298 Lakewood Dr.
P.O. Box 975
Luling, LA 70070

St. James Parish   (504) 869-3618
1542 Front St.
Rt. 1, Box 32-C
Lutcher, LA 70071
M-Th 8:30-6   F 8:30-5   S 8:30-1

St. John the Baptist Parish   (504) 652-6857
1334 W. Airline Highway
Riverlands Shopping Center
Laplace, LA 70068
M-Th 8:30-9   F-S 8:30-5:30

St. Landry Parish   (318) 948-3693
249 East Grolee St.
P.O. Box 249
Opelousas, LA 70570

St. Martin Parish   (318) 394-4086
105 S. New Market St.
P.O. Box 79
St. Martinville, LA 70582
M,W 8-8   T,Th,F 8-5   S 8-12

St. Mary Parish   (318) 828-5364
206 Iberia St.
Franklin, LA 70538

Terrebonne Parish   (504) 876-5861

424 Roussell St.
Houma, LA 70360
M-Th 9-8   F-S 9-5

Vermilion Parish   (318) 893-2655
200 North St.
P.O. Drawer 640
Abbeville, LA 70510

West Baton Rouge Parish   (504) 343-3484
830 N. Alexander
Port Allen, LA 70767
M-F 9-5:30   S 9-1

APPENDIX I

GENEALOGICAL SUPPLY COMPANIES

Genealogy Unlimited, Inc.   (800) 666-4363
P.O. Box 537
Orem, UT 84059-0537
Genealogy books, forms/charts, maps, organizational aids.

Everton Publishers, Inc.
P.O. Box 368
Logan, UT 84321
The Genealogical Helper magazine ($21/year; $4.50/issue).
Equipment and other supplies.

Barnette's Family Tree Company
1001 West Loop North
Houston, TX 77055
Genealogy books, forms/charts, supplies. Catalog ($1.00)

American Genealogical Lending Library (801) 298-5358
P.O. Box 244
Dept. M
Bountiful, UT 84011

Yearly subscription of $30 provides you with a catalog and allows you to rent/purchase their microfilms or microfiche. Cost per roll/fiche is less than $3. Two free rentals are included in the subscription fee. They also sell microfilm/microfiche viewing apparatus.

National Archives Microfilm Rental Program (301) 604-3699
P.O. Box 30
Annapolis Junction, MD 20701-0030

The $25 start-up fee gets you the catalogs of censuses and Revolutionary War material, several pamphlets, and two free rentals.

PUBLISHERS
Adams Press

25 E. Washington St.
Chicago, IL 60602

The Anundsen Publishing Co.   (319) 382-4295
108 Washington St.
P.O. Box 230
Decorah, IA 52101
Publications: *Your Manuscript in Print* --- $4

Dogwood Printing   (417) 485-8585
P.O. Box 716
Ozark, MO 65721

Family History Publishers (801) 295-7490
845 S. Main St.
Bountiful, UT 84010

Gateway Press, Inc.   (301) 837-8271
1001 N. Calvert St.
Baltimore, MD 21202
Publication: A Guide for Authors --- free

Genealogy Publishing Service   (704) 524-7063
448 Ruby Mine Road
Franklin, NC 28734
Publications: Services Brochure --- $1
How to Write and Publish Your Family Book --- $9.95

The Gregath Company   (800) 955-5232 ext. 355
P.O. Box 1045
Cullman, AL 35056-1045

McDowell Publications
11129 Pleasant Ridge Road
Utica, KY 42376
Publication: *Guidelines for Preparing a Book for Printing* --- $1

Professional Press
P.O. Box 3581

Chapel Hill, NC 27515-3581

Tennessee Valley Publishing   (800) 762-7079
Box 52527
Knoxville, TN 37950-2527
Publication: *Writing and Marketing a Family
History in the 1990s* --- $8.95

COMPUTER PROGRAMS

The Church of Jesus Christ of Latter-day Saints
Genealogical Society of Utah
35 North West Temple
Salt Lake City, UT 84150
Personal Ancestral File computer program ($35).

Commsoft, Inc.   (800) 327-6687
2257 Old Middlefield Way
Mountain View, CA 94043
ROOTS III computer program ($259) and accessory programs.
[Often available at a discount.]

Quinsept, Inc.   (800) 637-7668
P.O. Box 216
Lexington, MA 02173
Family Roots computer program ($225). (often available at a discount)

Genesis   (800) 346-0139
P.O. Box 640
Duvall, WA 98019-0640
Several cheap (less than $5) genealogy programs for IBM compatible
    computers.

The Software Labs   (800) 359-9998
3767 Overland Ave. 112-115
Los Angeles, CA 90034
Several cheap (less than $5) genealogy programs for IBM compatible
    computers.

APPENDIX J

LOUISIANA GENEALOGICAL TRAVEL GUIDE

1) New Orleans

Genealogical Locations

1. New Orleans Public Library 219 Loyola Avenue	504/596-2610
2. Howard-Tilton Library, Tulane University 6823 St. Charles Avenue	504/865-5605
3. Louisiana Historical Museum 400 Esplanade	504/568-6968
4. Historic New Orleans Collection 533 Royal Street	504/523-4662
5. Notarial Archives 421 Loyola Avenue	504/568-8577
6. Vital Records Louisiana State Office Building 325 Loyola Avenue	504/568-5152
7. Orleans Parish Courthouse	

Tourist Attractions

1. Audubon Zoo 6500 Magazine St.	504/861-2537
2. Aquarium of the Americas One Canal St.	504/861-2538
3. French Quarter Downtown New Orleans	

4. Jean Lafitte National Historical Park
916 N. Saint Peter St.   504/589-2636

5. Riverboat rides   504/586-8777

6. LA Nature & Science Center   504/246-5672
11000 Lake Forest Blvd.

7. LA Confederate Museum   504/523-4522
929 Camp St.

8. Shopping Malls
    Plaza Lake Forest (east New Orleans)
    5700 Read

    Riverwalk (downtown)
    One Poydras St.

    Esplanade (west of New Orleans, in Kenner)
    West Esplanade and Severn Ave.

2) Baton Rouge

Genealogical Locations

1. Louisiana State Library   504/342-4914
760 Riverside Dr.

2. Centroplex Library   504/389-4960
120 St. Louis St.

3. LSU Libraries, LSU

4. Louisiana State Archives   504/922-1207
3857 Essen Lane

5. East Baton Rouge Parish Courthouse

6. Division of State Lands   504/342-4586
Riverside Drive

Tourist Attractions

1. Rural Life Museum   504/765-2437
6200 Burden Lane

2. Baton Rouge Zoo   504/775-3877
Thomas Road

3. U.S.S. Kidd   504/342-1942
South River Road

4. LSU Museums, LSU

5. Shopping Malls
   Cortana (Airline and Florida Blvd.)
   Bon Marche (Florida Blvd.)

3) Lafayette

Genealogical Locations

1. Dupré Library, USL   318/231-6031

2. Lafayette Library   318/232-7567
301 West Congress St.

3. Lafayette Parish Courthouse

Tourist Attractions

1. Acadian Village   318/981-2364
200 Greenleaf Dr.

2. Vermilionville   318/233-4077
1600 Surrey St.   (800) 99-BAYOU

3. Shopping Malls

Acadiana (west Lafayette)
Northgate (north Lafayette)

4) Thibodaux
Genealogical Locations

1. Ellender Library, Nicholls State University   504/448-4646

2. Lafourche Parish Library   504/447-4119
314 St. Mary St.

3. Lafourche Parish Courthouse

Tourist Attractions

1. Laurel Valley Plantation   504/446-7456
Hwy 308, 2 miles below Thib.

2. Wetlands Division of the Jean Lafitte Nat'l Park   504/448-1375
Lafourche Parish Library
314 St. Mary St.

OTHER AREAS

Genealogical Locations

Each parish's courthouse and library has information of use to the genealogist. Also, colleges not previously listed usually have a section on Louisiana history and/or genealogy.

Tourist Attractions

Be sure to write to the Louisiana Office of Tourism for their Travel Guide. It contains hundreds of items from around the state, including the Acadiana area. It also gives the addresses of information centers around the state that can give you more detailed information. The address is:

Louisiana Office of Tourism
P.O. Box 94291
Baton Rouge, LA 70804-9291.

In Louisiana, their phone number is (504) 342-8119. Outside the state, you can use the 800 number, (800) 33-GUMBO.

Some of the attractions include: bayou cruises, museums, fishing, plantation homes, and a large variety of festivals.

APPENDIX K

ACADIAN GENEALOGICAL TRAVEL GUIDE

1) Nova Scotia

Genealogical Locations

1. Université Saint-Anne
   Located in southwest Nova Scotia where there is a high concentration of Acadian descendants.

2. Public Archives of Nova Scotia   902/424-6060
   6016 University Avenue
   Halifax, Nova Scotia B3H 1W4

Travel Locations

1. Grand Pré National Historic Site
   5 km east of Wolfville

2. Port Royal National Historic Site
   10 km from Annapolis Royal

3. Fort Anne National Historic Site
   Annapolis Royal

4. Fort Edward National Historic Site
   Windsor

5. Fortress of Louisbourg National Historic Site
   Louisbourg

6. Upper Clements Vacation Park   902/532-7557

P.O. 99
Clementsport, Nova Scotia B0S 1E0

7. Le Musée Acadian
West Pubnico

8. Cheticamp
A sizable Acadian population still resides here in northern Nova Scotia.

For more information, the Nova Scotia Dept. of Tourism puts out a comprehensive book and map that is loaded with details. Write to:

Nova Scotia Department of Tourism and Culture
P.O. Box 456
Halifax, Nova Scotia B3J 2R5

(Remember, postage to Canada is more than regular first class. Ask the post office for current rates.)

Help is also available via a toll free number. For information, call (800) 565-0000

2) New Brunswick

Genealogical Locations

1. Centre d'Etudes Acadiennes
Université de Moncton
Moncton, New Brunswick E1A 3E9

Travel Locations

1. Village Historique Acadien   506/727-3467
P.O. Box 820
Caraquet, NB E0B 1K0

A collection of Acadian homes from the nineteenth century. It is "inhabited" by locals who dress like nineteenth century Acadians and perform crafts of the era.

2. Acadien Museum   506/858-4088
   Université de Moncton

3. Survival of the Acadien National Historic Site
   Saint-Joseph de Memramcook

4. Fort Beausejour National Historic Park   506/536-0720
   Exit 55A on Trans-Canada Hwy

5. Aquarium & Marine Centre
   P.O. Box 1010
   Shipagan, New Brunswick E0B 2P0

6. Magic Mountain Amusement Park
   Moncton

For more information, the New Brunswick Department of Tourism puts out a comprehensive book and map that is loaded with details. Write to:

New Brunswick Department of Tourism, Recreation, and Heritage
P.O. Box 12345
Fredericton, New Brunswick E3B 5C3

(Remember, postage to Canada is more than regular first class. Ask the post office for current rates.)

Help is also available via a toll free number. For information, call (800) 561-0123.

3) Prince Edward Island

Genealogical Locations

1. Acadian Museum of P.E.I.   902/436-6237
   Rte. 2, 8 km west of Summerside

Contains a documentation center for genealogical research as well as a museum of Acadian materials.

2. Prince Edward Island Museum & Heritage Foundation
   Beaconsfield
   2 Kent Street
   Charlottetown, P.E.I.   C1A 1M6

Mostly the English, Irish, etc. history and genealogy.

Travel Locations

1. Acadian Pioneer Village   902/854-2227
   Rte. 11, west of Mont-Carmel
   A reproduction of an Acadian village of the early nineteenth century.

2. Mill River Fun Park   902/859-2071
   Mill River Fun Park Ltd.

3. The Great Island Adventure Park   902/886-2252
   Rte. 6

4. Fort Amherst/Port La Joye National Historic Site   902/675-2220
   Blockhouse Point Road

5. Micmac Indian Village   902/675-3800
   Rte. 19

For more information, the Prince Edward Island Department of Tourism puts out a comprehensive book and map that is loaded with details. Write to:

Visitor Services
P.O. Box 940
Charlottetown, Prince Edward Island C1A 7M5

(Remember, postage to Canada is more than regular first class. Ask the post office for current rates.)

Help is also available via a toll free number. For information, call (800) 565-0267.